WITHDRAWN

Radical feminism

Jesse Russell, Ronald Cohn

Publisher: LENNEX Corp
Pubmix is a trademark of LENNEX Corp,
Address: Mitchell house, 5 Mitchell Street, EDINBURGH, EH6 7BD, Scotland, United Kingdom
Email: info@pubmix.com
Website: www.pubmix.com

Published in 2012

Printed in: U.S.A., U.K., Germany, Spain, Russia, India, Brazil, China or Australia.

ISBN: 978-5-5110-9082-5

Contents

Articles

References

Article Licenses

Radical feminism

Radical feminism is a current theoretical perspective within feminism that focuses on the theory of patriarchy as a system of power that organizes society into a complex of relationships based on an assumption that "male supremacy"[1] oppresses women. Radical feminism aims to challenge and overthrow patriarchy by opposing standard gender roles and oppression of women and calls for a radical reordering of society.[1] Early radical feminism, arising within second-wave feminism in the 1960s,[1] typically viewed patriarchy as a "transhistorical phenomenon"[1] prior to or deeper than other sources of oppression, "not only the oldest and most universal form of domination but the primary form"[1] and the model for all others.[1] Later politics derived from radical feminism ranged from cultural feminism[1] to more syncretic politics that placed issues of class, economics, etc. on a par with patriarchy as sources of oppression.[1]

Radical feminists locate the root cause of women's oppression in patriarchal gender relations, as opposed to legal systems (as in liberal feminism) or class conflict (as in socialist feminism and Marxist feminism.)

Theory and ideology

Radical feminists in Western society assert that their society is a patriarchy in which men are the primary oppressors of women.[2] Radical feminists seek to abolish patriarchy. Radical feminism posits the theory that, due to patriarchy, women have come to be viewed as the "other" to the male norm and as such have been systematically oppressed and marginalized. They also believe that the way to deal with patriarchy and oppression of all kinds is to address the underlying causes of these problems through revolution.

While early radical feminists posited that the root cause of all other inequalities is the oppression of women, some radical feminists acknowledge the simultaneous and intersecting effect of other independent categories of oppression as well. These other categories of oppression may include, but are not limited to, oppression based on gender identity, race, social class, perceived attractiveness, sexual orientation, and ability.[3]

Patriarchal theory is not always defined as a belief that all men always benefit from the oppression of all women. Patriarchal theory maintains that the primary element of patriarchy is a relationship of dominance, where one party is dominant and exploits the other party for the benefit of the former. Radical feminists believe that men use social systems and other methods of control to keep non-dominant men and women suppressed. Radical feminists also believe that eliminating patriarchy, and other systems which perpetuate the domination of one group over another, will liberate everyone from an unjust society.

Some radical feminists called[4] for women to govern women and men, among them Andrea Dworkin,[5] Phyllis Chesler,[6] Monique Wittig (in fiction),[7] Mary Daly,[8] Jill Johnston,[9] and Robin Morgan.[10]

Redstockings co-founder Ellen Willis wrote in 1984 that radical feminism "got sexual politics recognized as a public issue",[1] "created the vocabulary... with which the second wave of feminism entered popular culture",[1] "sparked the drive to legalize abortion",[1] "were the first to demand total equality in the so-called private sphere"[1] ("housework and child care,... emotional and sexual needs"),[1] and "created the atmosphere of urgency"[1] that almost led to the passage of the Equal Rights Amendment.[1] The influence of radical feminism can be seen in the adoption of these issues by the National Organization for Women (NOW), a feminist group, that had previously been focused almost entirely on economic issues.[1]

The movement

Movement roots

The ideology of radical feminism in the United States developed as a component of the women's liberation movement. It grew largely due to the influence of the civil rights movement that had gained momentum in the 1960s and many of the women who took up the cause of radical feminism had had previous experience with radical protest in the struggle against racism. Chronologically, it can be seen within the context of second wave feminism, lasting from 1968 to 1973. The primary players and the pioneers of this second wave of feminism included the likes of Shulamith Firestone, Kathie Sarachild, Ti-Grace Atkinson, Carol Hanisch, and Judith Brown. Many local women's groups in the late sixties, such as the UCLA Women's Liberation Front (WLF), offered diplomatic statements of radical feminism's ideologies. UCLA's WLF co-founder Devra Weber recalls, "'... the radical feminists were opposed to patriarchy, but not necessarily capitalism. In our group at least, they opposed so-called male dominated national liberation struggles'".[11]

These women helped to make the connection that translated radical protest for racial equality over to the struggle for women's rights; by witnessing the discrimination and oppression to which the black population was subjected, they were able to gain strength and motivation to do the same for their fellow women. They took up the cause and advocated for a variety of women's issues, including abortion, the Equal Rights Amendment, access to credit, and equal pay.[12] While certainly worthy causes for advocacy, they failed to stir up enough interest among most of the women's fringe groups of society. A majority of women of color did not participate a great deal in the radical feminist movement because it did not address many issues that were relevant to those from a working class background, of which they were a sizeable part.[13] But for those who felt compelled enough to stand up for the cause, radical action was needed, and so they took to the streets and formed consciousness-raising groups to rally support for the cause and recruit people who would be willing to fight for it.

In the 1960s, radical feminism emerged simultaneously within liberal feminist and working class feminist discussions, first in the United States, then in the United Kingdom and Australia. Those involved had gradually come to believe that not only the middle-class nuclear family oppressed women, but also social movements and organizations that claimed to stand for human liberation, notably the counterculture, the New Left, and Marxist political parties, all of which they considered to be male-dominated and male-oriented. Women in countercultural groups related that the gender relations present in such groups were very much those of mainstream culture.

In the United States, radical feminism developed as a response to some of the perceived failings of both New Left organizations such as the Students for a Democratic Society (SDS) and feminist organizations such as NOW. Initially concentrated mainly in big cities like New York, Chicago, Boston, Washington, DC, and on the West Coast,[14] radical feminist groups spread across the country rapidly from 1968 to 1972.

In the United Kingdom, feminism developed out of discussions within community based radical women's organizations and discussions by women within the Trotskyist left. Radical feminism was brought to the UK by American radical feminists and seized on by British radical women as offering an exciting new theory. As the 1970s progressed, British feminists split into two major schools of thought: socialist and radical. In 1977, another split occurred, with a third grouping calling itself "revolutionary feminism" breaking away from the other two.

Australian radical feminism developed slightly later, during an extended period of social radicalization, largely as an expression of that radicalization.

As a form of practice, radical feminists introduced the use of consciousness raising (CR) groups. These groups brought together intellectuals, workers, and middle class women in developed Western countries to discuss their experiences. During these discussions, women noted a shared and repressive system regardless of their political affiliation or social class. Based on these discussions, the women drew the conclusion that ending patriarchy was the most necessary step towards a truly free society. These consciousness-raising sessions allowed early radical feminists to develop a political ideology based on common experiences women faced with male supremacy. Consciousness raising was extensively used in chapter sub-units of the National Organization for Women (NOW) during the 1970s.

The feminism that emerged from these discussions stood first and foremost for the liberation of women, as women, from the oppression of men in their own lives, as well as men in power. This feminism was radical in both a political sense (implying extremism), and in the sense of seeking the root cause of the oppression of women. Radical feminism claimed that a totalising ideology and social formation — *patriarchy* (government or rule by fathers) — dominated women in the interests of men.

Within groups such as New York Radical Women (1967–1969, no relation to Radical Women, a present-day socialist feminist organization), which Ellen Willis characterized as "the first women's liberation group in New York City",[1] a radical feminist ideology began to emerge that declared that "the personal is political"[1] and "sisterhood is powerful",[1] formulations that arose from these consciousness-raising sessions. New York Radical Women fell apart in early 1969 in what came to be known as the "politico-feminist split"[1] with the "politicos"[1] seeing capitalism as the source of women's oppression, while the "feminists"[1] saw male supremacy as "a set of material, institutionalized relations, not just bad attitudes."[1] The feminist side of the split, which soon began referring to itself as "radical feminists",[1] soon constituted the basis of a new organization, Redstockings. At the same time, Ti-Grace Atkinson led "a radical split-off from NOW",[1] which became known as The Feminists.[1] A third major stance would be articulated by the New York Radical Feminists, founded later in 1969 by Shulamith Firestone (who broke from the Redstockings) and Anne Koedt.[1]

During this period, the movement produced "a prodigious output of leaflets, pamphlets, journals, magazine articles, newspaper and radio and TV interviews."[1] Many important feminist works, such as Koedt's essay "The Myth of Vaginal Orgasm" (1970) and Kate Millet's book *Sexual Politics* (1970), emerged during this time and in this milieu.

Ideology emerges and diverges

At the beginning of this period, "heterosexuality was more or less an unchallenged assumption."[1] Among radical feminists, the view became widely held that, thus far, the sexual freedoms gained in the sexual revolution of the 1960s—in particular, the decreasing emphasis on monogamy—had been largely gained by men at women's expense.[1] This assumption of heterosexuality would soon be challenged by the rise of political lesbianism, closely associated with Atkinson and The Feminists.[1] The belief that the sexual revolution was a victory of men over women would eventually lead to the women's anti-pornography movement of the late 1970s.

Redstockings and The Feminists were both radical feminist organizations, but held rather distinct views. Most members of Redstockings held to a materialist and anti-psychologistic view. They viewed men's oppression of women as ongoing and deliberate, holding individual men responsible for this oppression, viewing institutions and systems (including the family) as mere vehicles of conscious male intent, and rejecting psychologistic explanations of female submissiveness as blaming women for collaboration in their own oppression.[15] They held to a view—which Willis would later describe as "neo-Maoist"[1]—that it would be possible to unite all or virtually all women, as a class, to confront this oppression by personally confronting men.[1]

The Feminists held a more idealistic, psychologistic, and utopian philosophy, with a greater emphasis on "sex roles",[1] seeing sexism as rooted in "complementary patterns of male and female behavior".[1] They placed more emphasis on institutions, seeing marriage, family, prostitution, and heterosexuality as all existing to perpetuate the "sex-role system".[1] They saw all of these as institutions to be destroyed. Within the group, there were further disagreements, such as Koedt's viewing the institution of "normal"[1] sexual intercourse as being focused mainly on male sexual or erotic pleasure, while Atkinson viewed it mainly in terms of reproduction.[1] In contrast to the Redstockings, The Feminists generally considered genitally focused sexuality to be inherently male.[1] Ellen Willis would later write that insofar as the Redstockings considered abandoning heterosexual activity, they saw it as a "bitter price"[1] they "might have to pay for [their] militance",[1] whereas The Feminists embraced separatism as a strategy.[1]

The New York Radical Feminists (NYRF) took a more psychologistic (and even biologically determinist) line. They argued that men dominated women not so much for material benefits as for the ego satisfaction intrinsic in domination. Similarly, they rejected the Redstockings view that women submitted only out of necessity or The Feminists' implicit view that they submitted out of cowardice, but instead argued that social conditioning simply led most women to accept a submissive role as "right and natural".[16]

Action

Radical feminism was not and is not only a movement of ideology and theory. Radical feminists also took direct action. In 1968, they protested against the Miss America pageant by throwing high heels and other feminine accoutrements into a garbage bin, to represent freedom.[17] In 1970, they also staged a sit-in at the *Ladies' Home Journal*.[18] In addition, they held speakouts[1] about topics such as rape.

Radical egalitarianism

Because of their commitment to radical egalitarianism, most early radical feminist groups operated initially without any formal internal structure. When informal leadership developed, it was often resented. Many groups ended up expending more effort debating their own internal operations than dealing with external matters, seeking to "perfect a perfect society in microcosm"[1] rather than focus on the larger world. Resentment of leadership was compounded by the view that all "class striving"[1] was "male-identified".[1] In the extreme, exemplified by The Feminists, the upshot, according to Ellen Willis, was "unworkable, mechanistic demands for an absolutely random division of labor, taking no account of differences in skill, experience, or even inclination".[1] "The result," writes Willis, "was not democracy but paralysis."[1] When The Feminists began to select randomly who could talk to the press, Ti-Grace Atkinson quit the organization she had founded.[1]

Social organization and aims in the U.S. and Australia

Radical feminists have generally formed small activist or community associations around either consciousness raising or concrete aims. Many radical feminists in Australia participated in a series of squats to establish various women's centres, and this form of action was common in the late 1970s and early 1980s. By the mid 1980s many of the original consciousness raising groups had dissolved, and radical feminism was more and more associated with loosely organized university collectives. Radical feminism can still be seen, particularly within student activism and among working class women.

In Australia, many feminist social organizations accepted government funding during the 1980s, and the election of a conservative government in 1996 crippled these organizations.

While radical feminists aim to dismantle patriarchal society in a historical sense, their immediate aims are generally concrete. Some common demands include:

• Expanding reproductive freedoms.

> "Defined by feminists in the 1970s as a basic human right, it includes the right to abortion and birth control, but implies much more. To be realised, reproductive freedom must include not only woman's right to choose childbirth, abortion, sterilisation or birth control, but also her right to make those choices freely, without pressure from individual men, doctors, governmental or religious authorities. It is a key issue for women, since without it the other freedoms we appear to have, such as the right to education, jobs and equal pay, may prove illusory. Provisions of childcare, medical treatment, and society's attitude towards children are also involved."[19]

• Changing the organizational sexual culture, *e.g.*, breaking down traditional gender roles and reevaluating societal concepts of femininity and masculinity (a common demand in U.S. universities during the 1980s). In this, they often form tactical alliances with other currents of feminism.

Other nations

The movement also arose in Israel among Jews.[20]

Radical feminism and Marxism

Some strains of radical feminism have been compared to Marxism in that they describe a "great struggle of history"[21] between two opposed forces. Much like the Marxist struggle between classes (typically, with reference to the present day, the proletariat and bourgeoisie), radical feminism describes a historical struggle between "women" and "men". Radical feminism has had a close, if sometimes hostile, relationship with Marxism since its origins.[1] Both Marxists and radical feminists seek a total and radical change in social relations and consider themselves to be on the political left. Despite this commonality, as ideologies Marxism and radical feminism have generally opposed one another; radical feminism can be contrasted to socialist feminism in this respect. In practice, however, activist alliances generally form around shared immediate goals.

Some radical feminists are explicitly avowed Marxists, and attempt to explore relationships between patriarchal and class analysis. This strain of radical feminism can trace its roots to the Second International (in particular, the Marxists Rosa Luxembourg and Alexandra Kollontai). These strains of radical feminism are often referred to as "Marxist feminism".

Other radical feminists have criticized Marxists; during the 1960s in the U.S., many women became feminists because they perceived women as being excluded from, and discriminated against by, leftist political groups.[22]

Feminist dominance in domestic violence discussions

The problems of interpersonal and domestic violence are often defined in a manner prescribed by feminist thought. Women's shelters for neglected or abused women and children now in place did not exist in the early 1970s. Laws mandating the reporting of domestic violence are now in place in all of the states of the U.S. Discussions of domestic violence are nearly always of a feminist construct, largely due to statistics that show women as having a higher rate of victimization.

> *Women experience significantly more partner violence than men do: 25 percent of surveyed women, compared with 8 percent of surveyed men, said they were raped and/or physically assaulted by a current or former spouse, cohabiting partner, or date in their lifetime; 1.5 percent of surveyed women and 0.9 percent of surveyed men said they were raped and/or physically assaulted by such a perpetrator in the previous 12 months. According to survey estimates, approximately 1.5 million women and 834,700 men are raped and/or physically assaulted by an intimate partner annually in the United States. Because women are also more likely to be injured by intimate partners, research aimed at*

understanding and preventing partner violence against women should be stressed.[23]

Sex-negative?

Both the self-proclaimed *sex-positive* and the so-called *sex-negative* forms of present-day feminism can trace their roots to early radical feminism. Ellen Willis' 1981 essay, "Lust Horizons: Is the Women's Movement Pro-Sex?" is the origin of the term, "pro-sex feminism". In it, she argues against making alliances with the political right in opposition to pornography and prostitution, as occurred, for example, during the Meese Commission hearings in the United States. Willis argued for a feminism that embraces sexual freedom, including men's sexual freedom, rather than condemn pornography, consensual BDSM, and in some cases sexual intercourse and fellatio.[24]

Criticisms

Within the New Left, radical feminists were accused of being "bourgeois", "antileft", or even "apolitical", whereas they saw themselves as further "radicalizing the left by expanding the definition of radical".[1] Radical feminists have tended to be white and middle class. Ellen Willis hypothesized in 1984 that this was, at least in part, because "most black and working-class women could not accept the abstraction of feminist issues from race and class issues";[1] the resulting narrow demographic base, in turn, limited the validity of generalizations based on radical feminists' personal experiences of gender relations.[1] Comedian George Carlin, in a routine from his 1990 HBO special *Doin' It Again*, remarked: "I've noticed that most of these feminists are white, middle class women. They don't give a shit about black women's problems, they don't care about Latino women, all they're interested in is their own reproductive freedom and their pocketbooks." Many early radical feminists broke political ties with "male-dominated left groups",[1] or would work with them only in *ad hoc* coalitions.[1]

Betty Friedan and other liberal feminists often see precisely the radicalism of radical feminism as potentially undermining the gains of the women's movement with polarizing rhetoric that invites backlash and hold that they overemphasize sexual politics at the expense of political reform. Other critics of radical feminism from the political left, including socialist feminists, strongly disagree with the radical feminist position that the oppression of women is fundamental to all other forms of oppression; these critics hold that issues of race and of class are as important or more important than issues about gender. Queer and postmodernist theorists often argue that the radical feminist ideas on gender are essentialist and that many forms of gender identity complicate any absolute opposition between "men" and "women".

Some feminists, most notably Alice Echols and Ellen Willis, held that after about 1975[1] most of what continued to be called "radical feminism" represents a narrow subset of what was originally a more ideologically diverse movement. Willis saw this as an example of a "conservative retrenchment"[1] that occurred when the "expansive prosperity and utopian optimism of the '60s succumbed to an era of economic limits and political backlash."[1] They label this dominant tendency "cultural feminism"[1] and view it as a "neo-Victorian"[1] ideology coming out of radical feminism but ultimately antithetical to it.[1] Willis drew the contrast that early radical feminism saw itself as part of a broad left politics, whereas much of what succeeded it in the 1970s and early 1980s (both cultural feminism and liberal feminism) took the attitude that "left politics were 'male' and could be safely ignored."[1] She further wrote that whereas the original radical feminism "challenge[d] the polarization of the sexes",[1] cultural feminism simply embraces the "traditional feminine virtues".[1] Critics of cultural feminism hold that cultural feminist ideas on sexuality, exemplified by the feminist anti-pornography movement, severely polarized feminism, leading to the "Feminist Sex Wars" of the 1980s. Critics of Echols and Willis hold that they conflate several tendencies within radical feminism, not all of which are properly called "cultural feminism", and emphasize a greater continuity between early and contemporary radical feminism.

Also, Willis, although very much a part of early radical feminism and continuing to hold that it played a necessary role in placing feminism on the political agenda, later criticised its inability "to integrate a feminist perspective with an overall radical politics,"[1] while viewing this limitation as inevitable in the historical context of the times.[1] In part this limitation arose from the fact that consciousness raising, as "the primary method of understanding women's condition"[1] in the movement at this time and its "most successful organizing tool",[1] led to an emphasis on personal experience that concealed "prior political and philosophical assumptions".[1]

Willis, writing in 1984, was critical of the notion that all hierarchies are "more specialized forms of male supremacy"[1] as preventing adequate consideration of the possibility that "the impulse to dominate... could be a universal human characteristic that women share, even if they have mostly lacked the opportunity to exercise it."[1] Further, the view of oppression of women as a "transhistorical phenomenon"[1] allowed middle-class white women to minimize the benefits of their own race and class privilege and tended to exclude women from history.[1] Further, Willis wrote that the movement never developed "a coherent analysis of either male or female psychology"[1] and that it ultimately raised hopes that its narrow "commitment to the sex-class paradigm"[1] could not fulfill; when those hopes were dashed, according to Willis the resulting despair was the foundation of withdrawal into counterculturalism and cultural feminism.[1]

Echols and Willis have both written that radical feminism was, ultimately, dismissive of lesbian sexuality. On the one hand, if the central struggle was to take place within personal heterosexual relationships, as envisioned by the Redstockings, lesbians were marginalized. On the other, political lesbianism granted lesbians a vanguard role, but only if they would play down erotic desire. Those lesbians whose sexuality focused on genital pleasure were liable to be dismissed by the advocates of political lesbianism as "male identified". The result, through the 1970s, was the adoption by many of a "sanitize[d] lesbianism", stripped of eroticism.[25]

References

[1] Willis, "Radical Feminism and Feminist Radicalism", p. 117.
[2] Alice Echols. *Daring to Be Bad: Radical Feminism in America 1967–1975*. University of Minnesota Press. p. 139. ISBN 0-8166-1787-2.
[3] Selma James, Sex, Race and Class (http://auto_sol.tao.ca/node/view/122), dated April 1, 2004 on the *Autonomy and Solidarity* website. Accessed online 7 July 2007.
[4] 1. Zerilli, Linda M. G., *Feminism and the Abyss of Freedom* (Chicago: Univ. of Chicago Press, 2005 (ISBN 0-226-98133-9)), p. 101.
     2. Eller, Cynthia, *The Myth of Matriarchal Prehistory: Why an Invented Past Won't Give Women a Future* (Boston, Mass.: Beacon Press, 2000 (ISBN 0-8070-6792-X)), p. 3.
[5] 1. Dworkin, Andrea, *Scapegoat: The Jews, Israel, and Women's Liberation* (N.Y.: Free Press, 2000 (ISBN 0-684-83612-2)), p. 246 and see pp. 248 & 336.
     2. *Take No Prisoners*, in *The Guardian*, May 13, 2000 (http://www.guardian.co.uk/books/2000/may/13/politics1), as accessed Sep. 6, 2010.
     3. Ouma, Veronica A., *Dworkin's Scapegoating*, in *Palestine Solidarity Review* (PSR), Fall 2005 (http://psreview.org/content/view/38/99/), as accessed Oct. 21, 2010.
[6] 1. Chesler, Phyllis, *Women and Madness* (N.Y.: Palgrave Macmillan, rev'd & updated ed., 1st ed. 2005 (ISBN 1-4039-6897-7)), pp. 335–336, 337–338, 340, 341, 345, 346, 347, & 348–349 (original ed. prob. published 1972, per *id.*, p. [ix] ("*1972 Acknowledgments*") (sales 2.5 million copies, per *id.* (pbk.), cover I, & Douglas, Carol Anne, Women and Madness, in *off our backs, op. cit.*).
     2. Douglas, Carol Anne, *Women and Madness*, in *off our backs*, vol. 36, no. 2, Jul. 1, 2006, p. 71, col. 1 (*Review*) (ISSN 00300071).
     3. Spender, Dale, *For the Record: The Making and Meaning of Feminist Knowledge* (London: The Women's Press, 1985 (ISBN 0-7043-2862-3)), p. 151 and see reply from Phyllis Chesler to author at p. 214.
[7] 1. Wittig, Monique, trans. David Le Vay, *Les Guérillères* (Boston, Mass.: Beacon Press, reprint 1985 (ISBN 0-8070-6301-0), © 1969 Les Editions de Minuit), *passim* and see pp. 112, 114–115, 127, 131, & 134–135 (novel).
     2. Moi, Toril, *Sexual/Textual Politics: Feminist Literary Theory* (London: Routledge, 2d ed., 2002 (ISBN 0-415-28012-5)), p. 78.
     3. Auerbach, Nina, *Communities of Women: An Idea in Fiction* (Cambridge, Mass.: Harvard Univ. Press, 1978 (ISBN 0-674-15168-2)), p. 186.
     4. Porter, Laurence M., *Feminist Fantasy and Open Structure in Monique Wittig's Les Guérillères*, in Morse, Donald E., Marshall B. Tymn, & Csilla Bertha, eds., *The Celebration of the Fantastic: Selected Papers from the Tenth Anniversary International Conference on the Fantastic in the Arts* (Westport, Conn.: Greenwood Press, 1992 (ISBN 0-313-27814-8)), p. 267.
     5. Zerilli, Linda M. G., *Feminism and the Abyss of Freedom, op. cit.*, p. 80 n. 51, quoting Porter, Laurence M., *Feminist Fantasy and Open Structure in Monique Wittig's Les Guérillères, op. cit.*, p. [261].
[8] Daly, Mary, *Gyn/Ecology: The Metaethics of Radical Feminism* (Boston, Mass.: Beacon Press, pbk. 1978 & 1990 (prob. all content except *New Intergalactic Introduction* 1978 & prob. *New Intergalactic Introduction* 1990) (ISBN 0-8070-1413-3)), p. 15 and see pp. xxvi & xxxiii (both in *New Intergalactic Introduction*) & pp. 29, 375 & fnn., & 384 (*New Intergalactic Introduction* separate from *Introduction: The Metapatriarchal Journey of Exorcism and Ecstasy*).
[9] 1. Johnston, Jill, *Lesbian Nation: The Feminist Solution* (N.Y.: Simon & Schuster, 1973 (SBN (not ISBN) 671-21433-0)), p. 248 and see pp. 248–249.
     2. Franklin, Kris, & Sara E. Chinn, *Lesbians, Legal Theory and Other Superheroes*, in *Review of Law & Social Change*, vol. XXV, 1999, pp. 310–311 (http://www.law.nyu.edu/ecm_dlv1/groups/public/@nyu_law_website__journals__review_of_law_and_social_change/documents/documents/ecm_pro_066374.pdf), as accessed Oct. 21, 2010 (citing in n. 45 *Lesbian Nation*, p. 15)).
     3. Ross, Becki L., *The House That Jill Built: A Lesbian Nation in Formation* (Toronto: Univ. of Toronto Press, pbk. 1995 (ISBN 0-8020-7479-0)), *passim*, esp. pp. 8 & 15–16 & also pp. 19, 71, 111, 204, 205, 212, 219, & 231.
     4. Ross, Becki L., *The House That Jill Built, op. cit.*, p. 204 & n. 18, citing McCoy, Sherry, & Maureen Hicks, *A Psychological Retrospective on Power in the Contemporary Lesbian-Feminist Community*, in *Frontiers*, vol. 4, no. 3 (1979), p. 67.
[10] Morgan, Robin, *Going Too Far: The Personal Chronicle of a Feminist* (N.Y.: Random House, 1st ed. 1977 (ISBN 0-394-48227-1)), p. 187.
[11] Linden-Ward, Blanche, and Carol Hurd Green. American Women in the 1960s: Changing the Future. (New York: Twayne Publishers, 1993) 418.
[12] Evans, Sarah M. "Re-viewing the Second Wave." Feminist Studies 28.2 (2002): 258-267. GenderWatch (GW). ProQuest. YRL, Los Angeles, CA. 23 Jan. 2008 <http://www.proquest.com/> 258.
[13] Linden-Ward and Green 434.
[14] Willis, "Radical Feminism and Feminist Radicalism", p. 118. Willis doesn't mention Chicago, but as early as 1967 Chicago was a major site for consciousness-raising and home of the *Voice of Women's Liberation Movement*; see Kate Bedford and Ara Wilson Lesbian Feminist Chronology: 1963-1970 (http://people.cohums.ohio-state.edu/wilson935/chrono1.htm), accessed online 8 July 2007.
[15] Willis, "Radical Feminism and Feminist Radicalism", p. 124–126.
[16] Willis, "Radical Feminism and Feminist Radicalism", p. 133–134.
[17] Alice Echols. *Daring to be Bad: Radical Feminism in America 1967-1975*. University of Minnesota Press. pp. 92–101. ISBN 0-8166-1787-2.
[18] Alice Echols. *Daring to be Bad: Radical Feminism in America 1967-1975*. University of Minnesota Press. pp. 195–197. ISBN 0-8166-1787-2.
[19] From *The Encyclopedia of Feminism* (1986) Lisa Tuttle
[20] Misra, Kalpana, & Melanie S. Rich, *Jewish Feminism in Israel: Some Contemporary Perspectives* (Hanover, N.H.: Univ. Press of New England (Brandeis Univ. Press), 1st ed. 2003 (ISBN 1-58465-325-6)) (author sr. fellow, Humphrey Institute of Public Affairs, Univ. of Minn., dir., Intntl. Women's Rights Action Watch, law degree, Univ. of Minn., & doctoral degree in Eng. & Am. lit., Univ. of Penna., editor Kalpana Misra assoc. prof. pol. sci., Univ. of Tulsa), & editor Melanie S. Rich psychologist & chair, Partnership 2000 Women's Forum).
[21] Catherine MacKinnon. *Toward a Feminist Theory of the State.*, 3.
[22] Alice Echols. *Daring to be Bad: Radical Feminism in America 1967-1975*. University of Minnesota Press. pp. 135–137. ISBN 0-8166-1787-2.

[23] From Prevalence, Incidence, and Consequences of Violence Against Women: Findings From the National Violence Against Women Survey. (http://www.ojp.usdoj.gov/nij/pubs-sum/172837.htm)

[24] Ellen Willis, Lust Horizons: The 'Voice' and the women's movement (http://villagevoice.com/specials/0543,50thewill,69320,31.html), *Village Voice* 50th Anniversary Issue, 2007. This is not the original "Lust Horizons" essay, but a retrospective essay mentioning that essay as the origin of the term. Accessed online 7 July 2007. A lightly revised version of the original "Lust Horizons" essay can be found in *No More Nice Girls*, p. 3–14.

[25] Willis, "Radical Feminism and Feminist Radicalism", p. 133, especially the citation of Alice Echols, "The New Feminism of Yin and Yang," in *Powers of Desire: the Politics of Sexuality*, ed. Christine Stansell, Ann Snitow and Sharon Thompson (Monthly Review Press, 1983).

Further reading

- Bell, Diane and Renate Klein. *Radically Speaking*. Spinifex Press ISBN 1-875559-38-8.
- Coote, Anna and Beatrix Campbell. (1987) *Sweet Freedom: The Movement for Women's Liberation*. Blackwell Publishers. ISBN 0-631-14957-0 (hardback) ISBN 0-631-14958-9 (paperback).
- Daly, Mary. (1978) *Gyn/Ecology: The Metaethics of Radical Feminism*. Beacon Pr. ISBN 0-8070-1413-3
- Firestone, Shulamith. (1970). *The Dialectic of Sex: The Case for Feminist Revolution*. William Morrow and Company. ISBN 0-688-06454-X (Reprinted editions: Bantam, 1979, ISBN 0-553-12814-0; Farrar Straus Giroux, 2003, ISBN 0-374-52787-3.)
- Koedt, Anne, Ellen Levine, and Anita Rapone, eds. (1973). *Radical Feminism*. Times Books. ISBN 0-8129-6220-6
- Love, Barbara J. and Nancy F. Cott. (2006). *Feminists Who Changed America, 1963–1975*. University of Illinois Press. ISBN 0-252-03189-X for biographies of participants in radical feminist groups
- MacKinnon, Catharine. (1989) *Toward a Feminist Theory of the State*. ISBN 0-674-89646-7
- Willis, Ellen, "Radical Feminism and Feminist Radicalism", 1984, collected in *No More Nice Girls: Countercultural Essays*, Wesleyan University Press, 1992, ISBN 0-8195-5250-X, p. 117–150.

External links

- Marxism, Liberalism, And Feminism (Leftist Legal Thought) (http://books.google.com/books?id=GrjPEY6yQNgC&printsec=frontcover&dq=eric+engle&hl=de&ei=_u7jTeCVLMTLswbWvpmLBg&sa=X&oi=book_result&ct=result&resnum=1&ved=0CDQQ6AEwAA#v=onepage&q&f=false) New Delhi, Serials (2010) by Dr.Jur. Eric Engle LL.M.
- *Notes from the First Year* (http://scriptorium.lib.duke.edu/wlm/notes/) – an early second-wave publication in which the development of a radical line can be traced.
- *Redstockings* (http://redstockings.org) – original source material available through radical feminists from Redstockings of the women's liberation movement.
- Strands of Feminist Theory (http://pers-www.wlv.ac.uk/~le1810/femin.htm) by Penny Welch, *Women's Studies, University of Wolverhampton*, February 2001.
- "Those Martian Women!" (http://web2.airmail.net/ktrig246/out_of_cave/martian.html) by Kathleen Trigiani, *Out of the Cave*, November 1999.
- "Radical Women in Gainesville, Florida" (http://www.uflib.ufl.edu/UFDC/?s=rwg&m=hitletter) by Leila Adams, 2008. A digital collection and online exhibit that documents the history of the radical women in Gainesville.
- Shapiro, Lynne (2010). "Radical Feminism: New York Radical Feminists revised history overview" (http://www.archive.org/details/RadicalFeminismNewYorkRadicalFeministsRevisedHistoryOverview) – a listing of the 1969–1977 activities and resources of the group New York Radical Feminists.

Anarcha-feminism

- A purple and black flag is often used to represent Anarcha-feminism.

- The symbol of Anarcha-feminism: in the center of the circle is a raised fist.

Anarcha-feminism (also called **anarchist feminism** and **anarcho-feminism**) combines anarchism with feminism. It generally views patriarchy as a manifestation of involuntary hierarchy. Anarcha-feminists believe that the struggle against patriarchy is an essential part of class struggle, and the anarchist struggle against the state. In essence, the philosophy sees anarchist struggle as a necessary component of feminist struggle and vice-versa. L. Susan Brown claims that "as anarchism is a political philosophy that opposes all relationships of power, it is inherently feminist".[1]

Origins

Anarcha-feminism was inspired by late 19th and early 20th century authors and theorists such as anarchist feminists Emma Goldman, Voltairine de Cleyre and Lucy Parsons.[2] In the Spanish Civil War, an anarcha-feminist group, Mujeres Libres ("Free Women") linked to the Federación Anarquista Ibérica, organized to defend both anarchist and feminist ideas,[3] while Stirnerist Nietzschean feminist Federica Montseny held that the "emancipation of women would lead to a quicker realization of the social revolution" and that "the revolution against sexism would have to come from intellectual and militant 'future-women.' According to this Nietzschean concept of Federica Montseny's, women could realize through art and literature the need to revise their own roles."[4]

The major male anarchist thinkers—with the exception of Proudhon—have strongly supported gender equality. Bakunin, for example, opposed patriarchy and the way the law "subjects [women] to the absolute domination of the man." He argued that "[e]qual rights must belong to men and women" so that women can "become independent and be free to forge their own way of life." Bakunin foresaw the end of "the authoritarian juridical family" and "the full sexual freedom of women." [Bakunin on Anarchism, p. 396 and p. 397].[5] Proudhon, on the other hand, viewed the family as the most basic unit of society and of his morality and thought women had the responsibility of fulfilling a traditional role within the family.[6]

Since the 1860s, anarchism's radical critique of capitalism and the state has been combined with a critique of patriarchy. Anarcha-feminists thus start from the precept that modern society is dominated by men. Authoritarian traits and values—domination, exploitation, aggression, competition, etc.—are integral to hierarchical civilizations and are seen as "masculine." In contrast, non-authoritarian traits and values—cooperation, sharing, compassion, sensitivity—are regarded as "feminine," and devalued. Anarcha-feminists have thus espoused creation of a non-authoritarian, anarchist society. They refer to the creation of a society, based on cooperation, sharing, mutual aid, etc. as the "feminization of society."[5]

Cover of *La Voz de la Mujer*, pioneering
Argentinian anarcha-feminist publication

In Argentina Virginia Bolten is responsible for the publication of a newspaper called *La Voz de la Mujer* (English: The Woman's Voice), which was published nine times in Rosario between 8 January 1896 and 1 January 1897, and was revived, briefly, in 1901. A similar paper with the same name was reportedly published later in Montevideo, which suggests that Bolten may also have founded and edited it after her deportation.[7]

Anarcha-feminism, individualist anarchism and the free love movement

Lucifer the Lightbearer, an influential American free love journal

An important current within individualist anarchism is free love.[8] Free love advocates sometimes traced their roots back to Josiah Warren and to experimental communities, which viewed sexual freedom as a clear, direct expression of an individual's self-ownership. Free love particularly stressed women's rights since most sexual laws discriminated against women: for example, marriage laws and anti-birth control measures.[8] The most important American free love journal was *Lucifer the Lightbearer* (1883–1907) edited by Moses Harman and Lois Waisbrooker[9] but Ezra and Angela

Heywood's *The Word* was also published from 1872–1890 and in 1892–1893.[8] Also M. E. Lazarus was an important American individualist anarchist who promoted free love.[8] In Europe the main propagandist of free love within individualist anarchism was Emile Armand[10] He proposed the concept of *la camaraderie amoureuse* to speak of free love as the possibility of voluntary sexual encounter between consenting adults. He was also a consistent proponent of polyamory.[10] In France there was also feminist activity inside French individualist anarchism as promoted by individualist feminists Marie Küge, Anna Mahé, Rirette Maitrejean, and Sophia Zaïkovska.[11]

Brazilian individualist anarchist Maria Lacerda de Moura lectured on topics such as education, women's rights, free love, and antimilitarism. Her writings and essays landed her attention not only in Brazil, but also in Argentina and Uruguay. In February 1923 she launched *Renascença*, a periodical linked with the anarchist, progressive, and freethinking circles of the period. Her thought was mainly influenced by individualist anarchists such as Han Ryner and Emile Armand.[12]

Maria Lacerda de Moura, Brazilian
individualist anarchist anarcha-feminist

Emma Goldman

Emma Goldman

Although she was hostile to first-wave feminism and its suffragist goals, Emma Goldman advocated passionately for the rights of women, and is today heralded as a founder of anarcha-feminism, which challenges patriarchy as a hierarchy to be resisted alongside state power and class divisions.[13] In 1897 she wrote: "I demand the independence of woman, her right to support herself; to live for herself; to love whomever she pleases, or as many as she pleases. I demand freedom for both sexes, freedom of action, freedom in love and freedom in motherhood."[14]

A nurse by training, Goldman was an early advocate for educating women concerning contraception. Like many contemporary feminists, she saw abortion as a tragic consequence of social conditions, and birth control as a positive alternative. Goldman was also an advocate of free love, and a strong critic of marriage. She saw early feminists as confined in their scope and bounded by social forces of Puritanism and capitalism. She wrote: "We are in need of unhampered growth out of old traditions and habits. The movement for women's emancipation has so far made but the first step in that direction."[15][16]

Mujeres Libres

Mujeres Libres (English: Free Women) was an anarchist women's organization in Spain that aimed to empower working class women. It was founded in 1936 by Lucía Sánchez Saornil, Mercedes Comaposada and Amparo Poch y Gascón and had approximately 30,000 members. The organization was based on the idea of a "double struggle" for women's liberation and social revolution and argued that the two objectives were equally important and should be pursued in parallel. In order to gain mutual support, they created networks of women anarchists. Flying day-care centres were set up in efforts to involve more women in union activities.[17]

In revolutionary Spain of the 1930s, many anarchist women were angry with what they viewed as persistent sexism amongst anarchist men and their marginalized status within a movement that ostensibly sought to abolish domination and hierarchy. They saw women's problems as inseparable from the social problems of the day; while they shared their comrade's desire for social revolution they also pushed for recognition of women's abilities and organized in their communities to achieve that goal. Citing the anarchist assertion that the means of revolutionary struggle must model the desired organization of revolutionary society, they rejected mainstream Spanish anarchism's assertion that women's equality would follow automatically from the social revolution. To prepare women for leadership roles in the anarchist movement, they organized schools, women-only social groups and a women-only newspaper so that women could gain self-esteem and confidence in their abilities and network with one another to develop their political consciousness.

Contemporary developments

An important aspect of anarcha-feminism is its opposition to traditional concepts of family, education and gender roles;[18] the institution of marriage is one of the most widely opposed.[19] De Cleyre argued that marriage stifled individual growth,[20] and Goldman argued that it "is primarily an economic arrangement... [woman] pays for it with her name, her privacy, her self-respect, her very life."[21] Anarcha-feminists have also argued for non-hierarchical family and educational structures, and had a prominent role in the creation of the Modern School in New York City, based on the ideas of Francesc Ferrer i Guàrdia.[22]

Young anarcha-feminists at an anti-globalization protest quote Emma Goldman

In English-speaking anarcha-feminist circles in the United States, the term "manarchist" emerged as a pejorative label for male anarchists who are dismissive of feminist concerns, who are overtly antifeminist, or who behave in ways regarded as patriarchal and misogynistic. The term was used in the 2001 article "Stick it To The Manarchy"[23] and later in a 2001 questionnaire, "Are You a Manarchist?".[24]

There is some concern that Anarcha-feminists in the developed world can be dismissive of third world feminist concerns. This has been noted especially in the plight of Anarcha-feminists in the Middle East. Contemporary anarcha-feminism has been noted for its heavy influence on ecofeminism. "Ecofeminists rightly note that except for anarcha-feminist, no feminist perspective has recognized the importance of healing the nature/culture division."[25]

Current Anarcha-feminist groups include Bolivia's Mujeres Creando, Radical Cheerleaders, the Spanish anarcha-feminist squat La Eskalera Karakola, and the annual La Rivolta! conference in Boston.

Contemporary anarcha-feminist writers/theorists include Peggy Kornegger, L. Susan Brown, the eco-feminist Starhawk and the post-left anarchist and anarcho-primitivist Lilith.[26] The vagabond feminist Valerie Solanas exposed anarcha-feminist views in her famous text SCUM Manifesto where she writes "Life in this society being, at best, an utter bore and no aspect of society being at all relevant to women, there remains to civic-minded, responsible, thrill-seeking females only to overthrow the government, eliminate the money system, institute complete automation and destroy the male sex."[27]

In the past decades two films have been produced about anarcha-feminism. *Libertarias* is a historical drama made in 1996 about the spanish anarcha-feminist organization Mujeres Libres. In 2010 the argentinian film *Ni dios, ni patrón, ni marido* was released which is centered on the story of anarcha-feminist Virginia Bolten and her publishing of the newspaper *La Voz de la Mujer* (English: The Woman's Voice)[28][29].

References

- Martha A. Ackelsberg, *Free Women of Spain: Anarchism and the Struggle for the Emancipation of Women* (AK Press: 2005)
- Susan Brown, "Beyond Feminism: Anarchism and Human Freedom", *Anarchist Papers 3* (Black Rose Books: 1990)
- Roxanne Dunbar-Ortiz, editor, *Quiet Rumours: An Anarcha-Feminist Reader* (Dark Star: 2002)
- Margaret S. Marsh, *Anarchist Women, 1870–1920* (1981)

Footnotes

[1] Brown, p. 208.
[2] Dunbar-Ortiz, p.9.
[3] Ackelsberg.
[4] Spencer Sunshine, "Nietzsche and the Anarchists" (http://radicalarchives.org/2010/05/18/nietzsche-and-the-anarchists/)
[5] An Anarchist FAQ. What is Anarcha-Feminism? (http://www.infoshop.org/faq/secA3.html)
[6] Broude, N. and M. Garrard (1992). *The Expanding Discourse: Feminism And Art History.* p. 303. Westview Press. ISBN 978-0064302074
[7] Molyneux, Maxine (2001). *Women's movements in international perspective: Latin America and beyond* (http://books.google.com/books?id=yg9HFrOG89kC&pg=PA24). Palgrave MacMillan. p. 24. ISBN 9780333786772. .
[8] The Free Love Movement and Radical Individualism By Wendy McElroy (http://www.ncc-1776.org/tle1996/le961210.html)
[9] Joanne E. Passet, "Power through Print: Lois Waisbrooker and Grassroots Feminism," in: *Women in Print: Essays on the Print Culture of American Women from the Nineteenth and Twentieth Centuries*, James Philip Danky and Wayne A. Wiegand, eds., Madison, WI, University of Wisconsin Press, 2006; pp. 229-50.
[10] E. Armand and "la camaraderie amoureuse[[Category:Articles containing French language text (http://www.iisg.nl/womhist/manfreuk.pdf)]." Revolutionary sexualism and the struggle against jealousy]
[11] "Individualisme anarchiste et féminisme à la « Belle Epoque »" (http://endehors.org/news/individualisme-anarchiste-et-feminisme-a-la-belle-epoque)
[12] "Maria Lacerda de Moura - Uma Anarquista Individualista Brasileira" by (http://www.nodo50.org/insurgentes/textos/mulher/09marialacerda.htm)
[13] Marshall, p. 409.
[14] Quoted in Wexler, *Intimate*, p. 94.
[15] Goldman, *Anarchism*, p. 224.
[16] See generally Haaland; Goldman, "The Traffic in Women"; Goldman, "On Love".
[17] Mujeres Libres - Women anarchists in the Spanish Revolution (http://flag.blackened.net/revolt/ws98/ws54_mujeres_libres.html)
[18] Emma Goldman, "Marriage and Love", in Alix Kates Shulman (ed.), *Red Emma Speaks: An Emma Goldman Reader*, Schocken Books, N.Y., 1982, pp. 204-13.
[19] Goldman, "Marriage and Love".
[20] Voltairine de Cleyre, They Who Marry Do Ill (http://dwardmac.pitzer.edu/Anarchist_Archives/bright/cleyre/theywhomarry.html) (1907)
[21] Goldman, "Marriage and Love", *Red Emma Speaks*, p. 205
[22] Paul Avrich, *The Modern School Movement: Anarchism and Education in the United States.*
[23] (http://onwardnewspaper.wordpress.com/volume-1-issue-2-spring-2001/stick-it-to-the-manarchy/)
[24] Are You A Manarchist? (http://www.anarcha.org/sallydarity/AreyouaManarchist.htm)
[25] Tuana, Nacy. Tong, Rosemarie. 'Feminism and Philosophy' Westview Press (1995) p. 328
[26] Lilith texts at the anarchist library (http://theanarchistlibrary.org/authors/Lilith.html)
[27] The S.C.U.M. Manifesto by Valerie Solanas (http://gos.sbc.edu/s/solanas.html)
[28] "Ni dios, ni patrón, ni marido" (2009) by Laura Mañá (http://www.cinenacional.com/peliculas/index.php?pelicula=7005)
[29] NI DIOS, NI PATRON, NI MARIDO - TRAILER (http://www.youtube.com/watch?v=LLh8AX0tcY0)

Further reading

- *Anarchism: A Documentary History of Libertarian Ideas - Volume One: From Anarchy to Anarchism (300CE-1939)*, ed. Robert Graham includes material by Louise Michel, Charlotte Wilson, Voltairine de Cleyre, Emma Goldman, Lucia Sanchez Soarnil (Mujeres Libres), and Latin American (Carmen Lareva), Chinese (He Zhen) and Japanese (Ito Noe and Takamure Itsue) anarcha-feminists.
- *On the Edge of All Dichotomies: Anarch@-Feminist Thought, Organization and Action, 1970-1983* (http://wesscholar.wesleyan.edu/etd_hon_theses/356/), by Lindsay Grace Weber; focuses on anarcha/o-feminism in the United States during the Second Wave of feminism.

External links

- Anarcha-feminism (http://www.dmoz.org/Society/Politics/Anarchism/Anarcha-Feminism//) at the Open Directory Project
- Anarcha- Communist Gender news (http://www.anarkismo.net/gender)
- anarcha-feminist articles at The anarchist library (http://theanarchistlibrary.org/topics/feminist.html)
- Anarcha-Feminism (http://www.infoshop.org/afem_kiosk.html) at Infoshop.org
- Anarcha (http://www.anarcha.org)
- Modern anarchist writings by women (http://www.struggle.ws/wsm/womenwriters.html)
- Libertarian Communist Library Archive (http://www.libcom.org/library)

D. A. Clarke

D. A. Clarke (also known as **De Clarke** and **DeAnander**) is a radical feminist essayist and activist in the United States of America since 1980. Much of her writing addresses the link between violence against women and market economics, although she may be best known for her 1991 essay "Justice Is A Woman with a Sword". In that essay, which she has updated twice for editions of the anthology *Transforming a Rape Culture*, she argues that feminist theory has taken a dogmatic approach to nonviolence and that women's self-defense, violent feminist activism, and the encouragement of positive media portrayals of violent women (such as in *Kill Bill* or *Xena: Warrior Princess*) have not been given the serious consideration they should receive and that their dismissal from mainstream feminism, while it may ultimately be desirable, has not been based on a properly thorough analysis. Her most popular work, however, may be the one least often correctly attributed to her: the early poem *privilege*, which has been found on dorm refrigerators and bulletin boards ascribed to 'Anonymous.' In this case, at least, Anonymous really was a woman.

In addition to being published in print anthologies, much of her work has appeared online. Clarke also had brief visibility as an amateur/indie musician, with one album "messages" released on cassette in the mid 80's.

Works by D.A. Clarke

Print Media

- editor/consultant for Stan Goff's book *Sex & War* 2006
- "Justice Is A Woman with a Sword: Some Thoughts on Women, Feminism, and Violence", essay published in *Transforming a Rape Culture* (ISBN 1-57131-269-2)
- "Prostitution for everyone: Feminism, globalisation and the 'sex' industry", essay published in *Not for Sale: Feminists Resisting Prostitution And Pornography* (ISBN 1-876756-49-7)
- "Consuming Passions: Some Thoughts on History, Sex, and Free Enterprise", essay published in *Unleashing Feminism: Critiquing Lesbian Sadomasochism in the Gay Nineties/a Collection of Radical Feminist Writings* (ISBN 0-939821-04-4)
- "Whose Tale is This?" film review of 'The Handmaid's Tale,' published in *off our backs* June 1990 p 12
- "Moving Expenses" short story published in Sinister Wisdom #38 (1989)
- *To Live With the Weeds* (Herbooks 1985, 1987) is a solo collection of poetry
- "Stack o Wheats: An Exercise in Issues" essay published in *Fight Back*, feminist anthology, eds. Delacoste and Newman, 1984
- "The Evidence of Pain" essay published in *Exposure* magazine, 1982

External links

- De Clarke's Personal Homepage [1]
- Feral Scholar [2] (Shared blog of Stan Goff and DeAnander)
- Lazy Quote Diary [3] (De Clarke's blog at European Tribune)
- U Dayton Discussion: R Whisnant class: Chat with readers of "Why is Beauty On Parade" [4] (archived at Archive.org)

Essays

- Feminista! : "Do Men *Need* Prostitution?" [5] (archived at Archive.org)
- Feminista! : "What is Feminism?" [6] (archived at Archive.org)
- Feminista! : "Necro-Feminism" (with J C Page) [7] (archived at Archive.org)
- NoStatusQuo: Justice Is A Woman With A Sword [8]
- NoStatusQuo: Consuming Passions: Some Thoughts on History, Sex, and Free Enterprise [9]
- NoStatusQuo: privilege: a poem for men who don't understand what we mean when we say they have it [10]
- Z Magazine: "Scandals of Sexual Greed: The Catholic Church and pedophiles" [11] (archived at Archive.org)
- The Nader Dilemma [12]
- What is Beauty Anyway? [13]
- Political Exposure: The Breast [14]

Interviews

- Out in the Redwoods: De Clarke [15], interview by Irene Reti, 2002.

References

[1] http://www.ucolick.org/~de/Personal.html
[2] http://www.feralscholar.org/blog/
[3] http://www.eurotrib.com/user/uid:20/diary
[4] http://web.archive.org/web/20050204024853/daclarke.org/UDayton.html
[5] http://web.archive.org/web/20071007160747/http://www.feminista.com/archives/v2n3/clarke.html
[6] http://web.archive.org/web/20071007160438/http://feminista.com/archives/v3n10/clarke.html
[7] http://web.archive.org/web/20071010113941/http://www.feminista.com/archives/v3n10/cutlerclarke.html
[8] http://www.nostatusquo.com/ACLU/Porn/Justice.html
[9] http://www.nostatusquo.com/ACLU/Porn/SexualFascism/dc/conpash.html
[10] http://www.nostatusquo.com/~de/banshee/privilege.html
[11] http://web.archive.org/web/20071024153915/http://zmagsite.zmag.org/oct2002/clarke1002.htm
[12] http://www.hartford-hwp.com/archives/45c/054.html
[13] http://www.mediawatch.com/wordpress/?p=16
[14] http://www.mediawatch.com/wordpress/?p=14
[15] http://library.ucsc.edu/reg-hist/oir.exhibit/de_clarke.html

Nikki Craft

Nikki Craft (born 1949) is an American political activist, radical feminist, artist and writer.

Activism

In 1975, she presented the Rockwell International Board of Directors with "...naked doll[s] splashed with blood-colored paint" to protest their B-1 bomber called "The Peacemaker".[1] The same year, Craft founded Women Armed for Self Protection (WASP), which advocated armed self-defense for women and retaliation against rapists by their victims; she wrote and recorded "The Rape Song" about Inez Garcia and Joan Little.[2]

In 1976, Craft co-founded the Kitty Genovese Women's Project (KGWP) when she and another activist posed as sociology students under the pretense of doing a "statistical study on violent crimes" and obtained the names of every indicted sex offender in Dallas County from 1959 to 1975. This was before such records were kept on computer; the activists worked for nine months writing all the names down on index cards. A year later, 25,000 copies of the KGWP newspaper were published. The paper listed all 2,100 sex offender indictments, 1,700 of which were multiple offenders, and was distributed throughout Dallas. On March 8, International Women's Day, the group read the names over local community radio KCHU for 13 hours.[3]

In 1979, Craft helped organize the first Myth California Anti-Pageant in Santa Cruz, California. In 1980 Craft joined other pageant protesters and over the next nine years conducted other actions, including throwing raw meat on the stage and pouring the blood of raped women across a pageant entryway. One year three men locked arms on stage, yelling "Men Resist Sexism! Men Resist Sexism!" preventing the crowning until they were dragged away. There were many arrests, and each year the crowds grew larger at the anti-pageant protests which later resulted in the Miss California pageant leaving Santa Cruz. The protests continued in San Diego and in 1988, after the pageant left Santa Cruz and moved to San Diego, the winner of a local pageant unveiled a banner from her bra at the state finals that read "Pageants Hurt All Women." A documentary called *Miss... or Myth?* examines these protests.[4]

1980s

Craft was arrested[5] in August 1984 while sunbathing at the Cape Cod National Seashore; she refused to put on her shirt.[6] She later organized a class action suit funded by the Naturist Society against the federal government, which manages the Seashore. Later in the proceedings, she and others withdrew from the case because the Society's attorney had made concessions to the respondents related to clothing requirements for Seashore visitors that included gender distinctions, specifically, the covering of women's breasts.

In 1986, Craft was arrested in Rochester, New York with six other women who were topless or "shirtfree" in public. The case was dismissed on appeal six years later, thus weakening the New York "exposure of a person" state law when pertaining to woman's breasts.[7][8][9]

1990s and onward

In 1990 Craft opened the Andrea Dworkin Online Library. In 1992, Diana E. H. Russell dedicated her book *Femicide* to Craft. In 1997 Dworkin dedicated her book *Life and Death* to Craft. In 2000, Craft and D.A. Clarke organized "Feminists for Nader [10]" and campaigned for Nader's presidential bid.

In 1995, the feminist journal *On the Issues* published Craft's article entitled "Busting Mister Short-Eyes" about a naturist child rapist sentenced to 30 years in prison, partly as a result of Craft's advocacy.[11]

In 2001 she protested the war in Afghanistan and called upon other feminists to do the same.[12] In 2005, she created the "Hustling the Left [13]" website, criticizing leaders in leftist and progressive movements who published articles, interviews and expressed public cooperation with Larry Flynt and his magazine, *Hustler*. The website took its name from a June 2005 article by feminist activist Aura Bogado, who protested the promotion of Flynt's support by the anti-war group Not in Our Name.

References

[1] *Wall Street Journal* Staff Reporter (1975-02-07). "Rockwell's B-1 Craft Proves to Be Bomb At Annual Meeting" (http://nostatusquo.com/ ACLU/Nikki/rockwell.html). . Retrieved 2009-03-21. Site article "War Stories: My Demo at Rockwell International" includes image/photocopy of original *Wall Street Journal* article. Exact date of the WSJ article is uncertain but either February 7 or 9, 1975.

[2] the Rape Song (http://www.nostatusquo.com/audio/rapesong.html)

[3] "Exposing the Rapist Next Door" (http://www.nostatusquo.com/ACLU/Porn/KGWP1.html). . Retrieved 2006-02-23. originally published in Seven Days Magazine, April 25, 1977 archived at No Status Quo (http://www.nostatusquo.com).

[4] Canby, Vincent (1987-09-16). "Movie Review — Miss... or Myth — Film: 'Gap-Toothed Women,' 'Miss . . . or Myth?' - NYTimes.com" (http://movies.nytimes.com/movie/review?res=9B0DE3D91531F935A2575AC0A961948260). *The New York Times*. . Retrieved 2009-03-23.

[5] Late City Final Edition (1984-08-26), "Topless Bather Arrested in Cape Cod Protest" (http://www.nytimes.com/1984/08/26/us/ topless-bather-arrested-in-cape-cod-protest.html), *New York Times*: 23,

[6] Late City Final Edition (1985-09-22), "Northeast Journal; Cape Cod Faces Nudity Question" (http://www.nytimes.com/1985/09/22/us/ northeast-journal-cape-cod-faces-nudity-question.html), *New York Times*: 50,

[7] Rochester Topfree Seven (http://www.tera.ca/legal.html#Rochester) 1992

[8] *Bodies of Law* by Alan Hyde, 1997, ISBN 0691012288, p. 141. Google books link (http://books.google.com/books?id=uun-6I-0b98C& pg=PA141&lpg=PA141&ots=RuxfBPynGJ&sig=EMkyZLy423jmyZEZgarl4o9pqfI#PPA140,M1)

[9] People v. Santorelli et al. (http://www.law.cornell.edu/nyctap/I92_0160.htm) 1992

[10] http://www.nostatusquo.com/Nader/index.html

[11] "Busting Mr. Short-Eyes" (http://www.nudisthallofshame.info/bustingmistershorteyes.pdf), *On The Issues, Winter 1995,*: 16–20 archived at The Nudist Naturist Hall of Shame (http://www.nudisthallofshame.info),

[12] "A Call On Feminists To Protest The War Against Afghanistan" (http://nostatusquo.com/ACLU/terrorism/terrorism1.html), *September 11, 2001: Feminist Perspectives*: 151–155, published in 2002 by Spinifex Press and archived at No Status Quo (http://www.nostatusquo. com),

[13] http://HustlingTheLeft.com

External links

- The Nikki Wiki: All About Nikki Craft (http://www.nikkicraft.com/) - Personal web site

Mujeres Creando

Mujeres Creando (*Eng: Women Creating*) is a Bolivian anarcha-feminist collective that participates in a range of anti-poverty work, including propaganda, street theater and direct action. The group was founded by María Galindo, Mónica Mendoza y J.Paredes in 1992 and members including two of Bolivia's only openly lesbian activists.

Mujeres Creando publishes *Mujer Pública* (*Eng: Public Woman*), produces a weekly radio show, and maintains a cultural café named Carcajada (*Eng: Laughter*).

Founder Julieta Paredes described Mujeres Creando as "a 'craziness' started by three women (Julieta Paredes, María Galindo and Mónica Mendoza) from the arrogant, homophobic and totalitarian Left of Bolivia during the 1980s, where heterosexuality was still the model and feminism was understood to be divisive."[1]

Mujeres Creando's *Mujer Publica*, May 2004

Mujeres Creando gained international attention due to their involvement in the 2001 occupation of the Bolivian Banking Supervisory Agency on behalf of Deudora, an organization of those indebted to microcredit institutions. The occupants, armed with dynamite and molotov cocktails, demanded total debt forgiveness and achieved some limited success. Julieta Ojeda, a member of Mujeres Creando, explains that "in reality the financial institutions were committing usury and extortion, cheating people and exploiting their ignorance, making them sign contracts that they didn't understand."[2] Mujeres Creando has denied that members directly participated in the occupation.[3]

On August 15, 2002 members of Mujeres Creando and supporters involved in the production of an educational film dealing with violence in relation to women's human rights were beaten by La Paz police. The police violence was condemned by the International Gay and Lesbian Human Rights Commission.[4]

References

[1] Paredes, Julieta (2002). *Quiet Rumors: An Anarch-Feminist Reader*. AK Press.

[2] "Mujeres Creando: An interview with Julieta Ojeda of Mujeres Creando" (http://www.zmag.org/ZMag/articles/jun02styles.html). *Z Magazine (June 2002)*. . Retrieved August 6, 2006.

[3] "Bolivia: debtors armed with dynamite and molotovs" (http://flag.blackened.net/revolt/ws/2001/66/bolivia.html). *Workers Solidarity (June 2002)*. . Retrieved August 6, 2006.

[4] "Video Crew Assaulted, Jailed: Defend The Right To Freedom Of Expression" (http://www.iglhrc.org/site/iglhrc/section.php?id=5&detail=46). *International Gay and Lesbian Human Rights Commission (August 2002)*. . Retrieved August 6, 2006.

External links

- Official Website - MujeresCreando.org (http://www.mujerescreando.org/) (in Spanish)
- *Mujeres Creando: An interview with Julieta Ojeda of Mujeres Creando* (http://www.zmag.org/ZMag/articles/jun02styles.html)
- *Mujeres Creando paints Bolivia* (http://www.americas.org/item_333), By Tom Kruse (1999)

Mary Daly

Mary Daly

Daly circa 1970	
Born	October 16, 1928 Schenectady, New York, U.S.
Died	January 3, 2010 (aged 81) Gardner, Massachusetts, U.S.
Era	20th century philosophy
Region	Western philosophy
School	Feminist philosophy
Main interests	Feminist theology, ontology, metaphysics

Mary Daly (October 16, 1928 – January 3, 2010[1][2]) was an American radical feminist philosopher, academic, and theologian. Daly, who described herself as a "radical lesbian feminist",[1] taught at Boston College, a Jesuit-run institution, for 33 years. Daly retired in 1999, after violating university policy by refusing to allow male students in her advanced women's studies classes. She allowed male students in her introductory class and privately tutored those who wanted to take advanced classes.[1][3][4]

Education

Before obtaining her two doctorates in sacred theology and philosophy from the University of Fribourg, Switzerland, she received her B.A. in English from The College of Saint Rose, her M.A. in English from The Catholic University of America, and a doctorate in religion from Saint Mary's College.

Career

Daly taught classes at Boston College from 1967 to 1999, including courses in theology, feminist ethics, and patriarchy.

Daly was first threatened with dismissal when, following the publication of her first book, *The Church and the Second Sex* (1968), she was issued a terminal contract. As a result of support from the (then all-male) student body and the general public, however, Daly was ultimately granted tenure.

Daly's refusal to admit male students to some of her classes at Boston College also resulted in disciplinary action. While Daly argued that their presence inhibited class discussion, Boston College took the view that her actions were in violation of title IX of federal law requiring the College to ensure that no person was excluded from an education program on the basis of sex, and of the University's own non-discrimination policy insisting that all courses be open to both male and female students.

In 1998, a discrimination claim against the college by two male students was backed by the Center for Individual Rights, a conservative advocacy group. Following further reprimand, Daly absented herself from classes rather than admit the male students.[5] Boston College removed her tenure rights, citing a verbal agreement by Daly to retire. She brought suit against the college disputing violation of her tenure rights and claimed she was forced out against her will, but her request for an injunction was denied by Middlesex Superior Court Judge Martha Sosman.[6]

A confidential out-of-court settlement was reached. The college maintains that Daly had agreed to retire from her faculty position,[7] while others assert she was forced out.[8][9] Daly maintained that Boston College wronged her students by depriving her of her right to teach freely to only female students.[10] She documented her account of the events in the 2006 book, *Amazon Grace: Recalling the Courage to Sin Big*.

Daly protested the commencement speech of Condoleezza Rice at Boston College, and she spoke on campuses around the United States as well as internationally.[11]

Works

Daly published a number of works, and is perhaps best known for her second book, *Beyond God the Father* (1973). *Beyond God the Father* is the last book in which Daly really considers God a substantive subject. She laid out her systematic theology, following Paul Tillich's example.[12] Often regarded as a foundational work in feminist theology, *Beyond God the Father* is her attempt to explain and overcome androcentrism in Western religion, and it is notable for its playful writing style and its attempt to rehabilitate "God-talk" for the women's liberation movement by critically building on the writing of existentialist theologians such as Paul Tillich and Martin Buber. While the former increasingly characterized her writing, she soon abandoned the latter.

Daly's *Gyn/Ecology: The Metaethics of Radical Feminism* (1978) argues that men throughout history have sought to oppress women. In this book she moves beyond her previous thoughts on the history of patriarchy to the focus on the actual practices that, in her view, perpetuate patriarchy, which she calls a religion.[12]

Daly's *Pure Lust: Elemental Feminist Philosophy* (1984) and *Webster's First New Intergalactic Wickedary of the English Language* (1987) introduce and explore an alternative language to explain the process of exorcism and ecstasy. In *Wickedary* Daly provides definitions as well as chants that she says can be used by women to free themselves from patriarchal oppression. She also explores the labels that she says patriarchal society places on women to prolong what she sees as male domination of society. Daly said it is the role of women to unveil the liberatory nature of labels such as "Hag", "Witch", and "Lunatic".[13]

Daly's work continues to influence feminism and feminist theology, as well as the developing concept of biophilia as an alternative and challenge to social necrophilia. She was an ethical vegetarian and animal rights activist. *Gyn/Ecology*, *Pure Lust*, and *Webster's First New Intergalactic Wickedary* all endorse anti-vivisection and anti-fur positions. Daly was a member of the advisory board of Feminists For Animal Rights, a group which is now defunct.

Daly created her own theological anthropology based around the context of what it means to be a woman. She created a dualistic thought-praxis that separates the world into the world of false images that create oppression and the world of communion in true being. She labeled these two areas Foreground and Background respectively. Daly considered the Foreground the realm of patriarchy and the Background the realm of Woman. She argued that the Background is under and behind the surface of the false reality of the Foreground. The Foreground, for Daly, was a distortion of true being, the paternalistic society in which she said most people live. It has no real energy, but drains the "life energy" of women residing in the Background. In her view, the Foreground creates a world of poisons that contaminate natural life. She called the male-centered world of the Foreground necrophilic, hating all living things. In contrast, she conceived of the Background as a place where all living things connect.[13][14]

Gyn/Ecology

Audre Lorde expressed concern over *Gyn/Ecology*, citing homogenizing tendencies, and a refusal to acknowledge the "herstory and myth" of women of color.[15] The letter,[16] and Daly's apparent decision not to publicly respond, greatly affected the reception of Daly's work among other feminist theorists, and has been described as a "paradigmatic example of challenges to white feminist theory by feminists of color in the 1980s."[14]

Daly's reply letter to Lorde,[17] dated 4½ months later, was found in 2003 in Lorde's files after she died.[18] Daly's reply was followed in a week by a meeting with Lorde at which Ms. Daly said, among other things, that *Gyn/Ecology* was not a compendium of goddesses but limited to "those goddess myths and symbols that were direct sources of Christian myth," but whether this was accepted by Ms. Lorde was unknown at the time.[19]

Views on men

She argued against sexual equality,[20] believing that women ought to govern men;[21] Daly advocated a reversal of sociopolitical power between the sexes.[22]

In an interview with *What Is Enlightenment?* magazine, Daly said, "*I don't think about men.* I really don't care about them. I'm concerned with *women's* capacities, which have been infinitely diminished under patriarchy. Not that they've disappeared, but they've been made subliminal. I'm concerned with *women* enlarging our capacities, actualizing them. So that takes all my energy."[23]

Later in the interview, she said, "If life is to survive on this planet, there must be a decontamination of the Earth. I think this will be accompanied by an evolutionary process that will result in a drastic reduction of the population of males."[23]

Views on transsexualism

In *Gyn/Ecology,* Daly asserted her negative view of transsexual people, writing, "Today the Frankenstein phenomenon is omnipresent . . . in . . . phallocratic technology. . . . Transsexualism is an example of male surgical siring which invades the female world with substitutes."[24] "Transsexualism, which Janice Raymond has shown to be essentially a male problem, is an *attempt* to change males into females, whereas in fact no male can assume female chromosomes and life history/experience."[25] "The surgeons and hormone therapists of the transsexual kingdom . . . can be said to produce feminine persons. They cannot produce women."[26]

Daly was also the dissertation advisor to Janice Raymond, whose dissertation, published in 1979 as *The Transsexual Empire*, is critical of transsexualism.

Bibliography

Books

* *The Church and the Second Sex.* Harper & Row, 1968. OCLC 1218746
* *Beyond God the Father: Toward a Philosophy of Women's Liberation.* Beacon Press, 1973. ISBN 0807027685
* *Gyn/Ecology: The Metaethics of Radical Feminism.* Beacon Press, 1978. ISBN 0807015105
* *Pure Lust: Elemental Feminist Philosophy.* Beacon Press, 1984. ISBN 0807015040
* *Websters' First New Intergalactic Wickedary of the English Language, Conjured in Cahoots with Jane Caputi* (with Jane Caputi and Sudie Rakusin). Beacon Press, 1987. ISBN 0807067067
* *Outercourse: The Bedazzling Voyage, Containing Recollections from My Logbook of a Radical Feminist Philosopher.* HarperSanFrancisco, 1992. ISBN 0062501941
* *Quintessence... Realizing the Archaic Future: A Radical Elemental Feminist Manifesto.* Beacon Press, 1998. ISBN 0807067903
* *Amazon Grace: Re-Calling the Courage to Sin Big.* Palgrave Macmillan, 1st ed. Jan. 2006. ISBN 1403968535

Articles

* *The Spiritual Dimension of Women's Liberation.* In *Notes From The Third Year: Women's Liberation*, 1971.[27]
* *A Call for the Castration of Sexist Religion.* In *The Unitarian Universalist Christian* 27 (Autumn/Winter 1972), pp. 23–37.
* *God Is A Verb.* In *Ms.,* (Dec., 1974), pp. 58–62, 96-98.
* *Prelude to the First Passage.* In *Feminist Studies,* vol. 4, no. 3 (Oct., 1978), pp. 81–86. Text is from *Gyn/Ecology* (book), at the time not yet published.
* *Sin Big.* In *The New Yorker* (Feb 26 & Mar 4, 1996), pp. 76–84.

Theses/Dissertations

* *Natural Knowledge of God in the Philosophy of Jacques Maritain.* Officium Libri Catholici, 1966. OCLC 2219525
* *The Problem of Speculative Theology.* Thomist Press. 1965. OCLC (4 records) [28]

References

[1] Fox, Margalit (January 6, 2010). "Mary Daly, a Leader in Feminist Theology, Dies at 81" (http://www.nytimes.com/2010/01/07/ education/07daly.html?hpw). The New York Times. . Retrieved January 7, 2010.
[2] Fox, Thomas C. (January 4, 2010). "Feminist theologian Mary Daly dies" (http://ncronline.org/blogs/ncr-today/ feminist-theologian-mary-daly-dies). *National Catholic Reporter*. . Retrieved January 4, 2010.
[3] "Feminist BC theology professor Mary Daly dies" (http://www.bostonherald.com/news/regional/view/ 20100106feminist_bc_theology_professor_mary_daly_dies/srvc=home&position=recent). *Associated Press*. 6 January 2010. . Retrieved 13 January 2010.
[4] Madsen, Catherine (Fall 2000). "The Thin Thread of Conversation: An Interview with Mary Daly" (http://www.crosscurrents.org/ madsenf00.htm). *Cross Currents*. . Retrieved January 13, 2010.
[5] Seele, Michael (March 4, 1999). "Daly's Absence Prompts Cancellations" (http://www.bc.edu/bc_org/rvp/pubaf/chronicle/v7/mr4/ daly.html). The Boston College Chronicle. .
[6] Sullivan, Mark (May 28, 1999). "Judge Denies Daly's Bid for Injunction" (http://www.bc.edu/bc_org/rvp/pubaf/chronicle/v7/my28/ daly.html). The Boston College Chronicle. .
[7] "Mary Daly Ends Suit, Agrees to Retire" (http://www.bc.edu/bc_org/rvp/pubaf/chronicle/v9/f15/daly.html). The Boston College Chronicle. February 15, 2001. .
[8] Pippin, Tina (2009). "Mary Daley" (http://books.google.com/books?id=u-_6P2rMy2wC&pg=PA326). In Queen II, Edward L.; Prothero, Stephen R.; Shattuck, Jr., Gardiner H.. *Encyclopedia of American Religious History*. **3** (3d ed.). New York: Facts on File. p. 326. ISBN 978-0-8160-6660-5. . Retrieved August 25, 2011.

[9] Thistlethwaite, Susan Brooks (January 5, 2010). "Mary Daly's 'Courage to Sin Big'" (http://newsweek.washingtonpost.com/onfaith/panelists/susan_brooks_thistlethwaite/2010/01/the_courage_to_sin_big_the_life_of_mary_daly.html). *The Washington Post.* . Retrieved August 25, 2011.

[10] Kettle, Martin (February 27, 1999). "Unholy row as feminist lecturer bars men" (http://www.guardian.co.uk/world/1999/feb/27/martinkettle). The Guardian. .

[11] Elton, Catherine (May 9, 2006). "Efforts mount against BC's Rice invitation" (http://www.boston.com/news/local/articles/2006/05/09/efforts_mount_against_bcs_rice_invitation/). The Boston Globe. .

[12] Riswold, Caryn D. (2007). *Two Reformers.* Eugene, OR: Wipf & Stock Publishers. pp. 33. ISBN 1597528269.

[13] Ruether, Rosemary Radford (1998). *Women and Redemption: A Theological History.* Minneapolis: Fortress Press. pp. 218–9. ISBN 0800629477.

[14] Hoagland, Sarah Lucia; Frye, Marilyn (2000), *Feminist interpretations of Mary Daly*, Penn State Press, pp. 60, 267, ISBN 0271020199

[15] Audre, Lorde (1984). *An Open Letter to Mary Daly.* Berkeley: Crossing Press. pp. 66–71.

[16] Audre Lorde's letter is discussed in Dr. Daly's book, *Outercourse*.

[17] *Amazon Grace* (N.Y.: Palgrave Macmillan, 1st ed. [1st printing?] Jan. 2006), pp. 25–26 (reply text).

[18] *Amazon Grace*, supra, pp. 22–26, esp. pp. 24–26 & nn. 15–16, citing *Warrior Poet: A Biography of Audre Lorde*, by Alexis De Veaux (N.Y.: W.W. Norton, 1st ed. 2004) (ISBN 0393019543 or ISBN 0393329356).

[19] See *Amazon Grace*, supra, p. 23 ("week" per pp. 24 & 23).

[20] Daly, Mary, *Gyn/Ecology: The Metaethics of Radical Feminism* (Boston, Mass.: Beacon Press, 1978 & 1990), pp. 384 & 375–376 (fnn. omitted) (prob. all content except *New Intergalactic Introduction* 1978 & prob. *New Intergalactic Introduction* 1990) (ISBN 0-8070-1413-3)) (*New Intergalactic Introduction* is separate from *Introduction: The Metapatriarchal Journey of Exorcism and Ecstasy*).

[21] Daly, Mary, *Gyn/Ecology: The Metaethics of Radical Feminism*, pp. 15 & xxvi (p. xxvi in *New Intergalactic Introduction* (prob. 1990)).

[22] Daly, Mary, *Gyn/Ecology: The Metaethics of Radical Feminism*, p. xxvi (*New Intergalactic Introduction* (prob. 1990)).

[23] Bridle, Susan (Fall/Winter 1999). "No Man's Land". EnlightenNext Magazine.

[24] Daly, Mary, *Gyn/Ecology: The Metaethics of Radical Feminism* (Boston, Mass.: Beacon Press, pbk. [1st printing? printing of [19]90?] 1978 & 1990 (prob. all content except *New Intergalactic Introduction* 1978 & prob. *New Intergalactic Introduction* 1990) (ISBN 0-8070-1413-3)), pp. 70–71 (page break within ellipsis between sentences) (*New Intergalactic Introduction* is separate from *Introduction: The Metapatriarchal Journey of Exorcism and Ecstasy*).

[25] Daly, Mary, *Gyn/Ecology, op. cit.*, p. 238 n.

[26] Daly, Mary, *Gyn/Ecology, op. cit.*, p. 68 (n. 60 (at end) omitted).

[27] In *Notes From The Third Year: Women's Liberation* (N.Y.: Notes from the Second Year, Inc., 1971), pp. 75–79.

[28] http://www.worldcat.org/search?q=%22The+Problem+of+Speculative+Theology%22&qt=owc_search

Further reading

- Marquard, Bryan (January 5, 2010). "Mary Daly, pioneering feminist who tussled with BC, dies at 81" (http://www.boston.com/news/local/breaking_news/2010/01/mary_daly_pione.html). *The Boston Globe.* Retrieved January 5, 2010.
- Ring, Trudy (January 5, 2010). "Mary Daly Dead at 81" (http://www.advocate.com/article.aspx?id=105004). *The Advocate.* Retrieved January 5, 2010.

External links

- Works by or about Mary Daly (http://worldcat.org/identities/lccn-n50-38985) in libraries (WorldCat catalog)
- Bibliography, Feminist Theory Website, by Kristin Switala et al., hosted at Center for Digital Discourse and Culture (CDDC), Virginia Tech University (http://www.cddc.vt.edu/feminism/Daly.html) (bibliography includes many articles)
- New York University website re "Wickedary" (http://cat.nyu.edu/wickedary/dalyinfo.html)
- Hagerty, Barbara Bradley (January 5, 2010). "Feminist Theologian Mary Daly Remembered" (http://www.npr.org/templates/story/story.php?storyId=122258110) (MP3). NPR. Retrieved January 5, 2010.
- Mary Daly on the GLBTQ encyclopedia (http://www.glbtq.com/social-sciences/daly_m.html) (biography)
- Interview with Mary Daly on KDVS, April 5 2006 (http://www.archive.org/details/KDVS_The_Fringe_4-5-06)
- "Mary Daly." Encyclopædia Britannica. Encyclopædia Britannica Online. Encyclopædia Britannica Inc., 2011. Web. 10 Nov. 2011. <http://www.britannica.com/EBchecked/topic/1655663/Mary-Daly>.

Andrea Dworkin

Andrea Dworkin	
Born	Andrea Rita Dworkin September 26, 1946 Camden, New Jersey, U.S.
Died	April 9, 2005 (aged 58) Washington, D.C., U.S.
Cause of death	Myocarditis
Education	B.A. in literature
Alma mater	Bennington College
Occupation	Writer
Years active	1966–2005
Known for	Radical feminism, anti-pornography activism
Spouse	Cornelius (Iwan) Dirk de Bruin (1969–1972) John Stoltenberg
Parents	Harry Dworkin and Sylvia Spiegel
Relatives	Mark Spiegel (brother)
Website	
Portal for Andrea Dworkin's websites [1]	

Andrea Rita Dworkin (September 26, 1946 – April 9, 2005) was an American radical feminist and writer best known for her criticism of pornography, which she argued was linked to rape and other forms of violence against women.

An anti-war activist and anarchist in the late 1960s, Dworkin wrote 10 books on radical feminist theory and practice. During the late 1970s and the 1980s, she gained national fame as a spokeswoman for the feminist anti-pornography movement, and for her writing on pornography and sexuality, particularly in *Pornography: Men Possessing Women* (1981) and *Intercourse* (1987), which remain her two most widely known books.

Early life and education

Dworkin was born in Camden, New Jersey, to Harry Dworkin and Sylvia Spiegel. She had one younger brother, Mark. Her father was a schoolteacher and dedicated socialist, whom she credited with inspiring her passion for social justice. Her relationship with her mother was strained, but Dworkin later wrote about how her mother's belief in legal birth control and legal abortion, "long before these were respectable beliefs," inspired her later activism.[2]

Though she described her Jewish household as being in many ways dominated by the memory of the Holocaust, it nonetheless provided a happy childhood until the age of nine when an unknown man molested her in a movie theater. When Dworkin was 10, her family moved from the city to the suburbs of Cherry Hill, New Jersey (then known as Delaware Township), which she later wrote she "experienced as being kidnapped by aliens and taken to a penal colony".[3] In sixth grade, the administration at her new school punished her for refusing to sing "Silent Night" (as a Jew, she objected to being forced to sing Christian religious songs at school).[4]

Dworkin began writing poetry and fiction in the sixth grade. Throughout high school, she read avidly, with encouragement from her parents. She was particularly influenced by Arthur Rimbaud, Charles Baudelaire, Henry Miller, Fyodor Dostoevsky, Che Guevara, and the Beat poets, especially Allen Ginsberg.[5]

She was married 1969–1972 to Cornelius (Iwan) Dirk de Bruin.[6]

College and early activism

In 1965, while a student at Bennington College, Dworkin was arrested during an anti-Vietnam War protest at the United States Mission to the United Nations and sent to the New York Women's House of Detention. Dworkin testified that the doctors in the House of Detention gave her an internal examination which was so rough that she bled for days afterwards. She spoke in public and testified before a grand jury about her experience, and the media coverage of her testimony made national and international news.[7] The grand jury declined to make an indictment in the case,[8] but Dworkin's testimony contributed to public outrage over the mistreatment of inmates. The prison was closed seven years later.

Soon after testifying before the grand jury, Dworkin left Bennington to live in Greece and to pursue her writing.[9] She traveled from Paris to Athens on the Orient Express, and went to live and write in Crete.[10] While in Crete, she wrote a series of poems titled *(Vietnam) Variations*, a collection of poems and prose poems that she printed on the island in a book called *Child*, and a novel in a style resembling magical realism called *Notes on Burning Boyfriend* -- a reference to the pacifist Norman Morrison, who had burned himself to death in protest of the Vietnam War. She also wrote several poems and dialogues which she hand-printed after returning to the United States in a book called *Morning Hair*.[11]

After living in Crete, Dworkin returned to Bennington for two years, where she continued to study literature and participated in campaigns against the college's student conduct code, for contraception on campus, for the legalization of abortion, and against the Vietnam War.[12] She graduated with a degree in literature in 1968.

Life in the Netherlands

After graduation, she moved to Amsterdam to interview Dutch anarchists in the Provo countercultural movement.[13] While there, she became involved with, then married, one of the anarchists she met. Soon after they were married, she said, he began to abuse her severely, punching and kicking her, burning her with cigarettes, beating her on her legs with a wooden beam, and banging her head against the floor until he knocked her unconscious.[14]

After she left her husband late in 1971, Dworkin said, her ex-husband attacked, persecuted, and harassed her, beating her and threatening her whenever he found where she was hiding. She found herself desperate for money, often homeless, thousands of miles from her family, later remarking that, "I often lived the life of a fugitive, except that it was the more desperate life of a battered woman who had run away for the last time, whatever the outcome".[15] For a while, she was a prostitute. Ricki Abrams, a feminist and fellow expatriate, sheltered Dworkin in her home, and helped her find places to stay on houseboats, a communal farm, and deserted buildings.[16] Dworkin tried to work up the money to return to the United States.

Abrams introduced Dworkin to early radical feminist writing from the United States, and Dworkin was especially inspired by Kate Millett's *Sexual Politics*, Shulamith Firestone's *The Dialectic of Sex*, and Robin Morgan's *Sisterhood is Powerful*.[17] She and Abrams began to work together on "early pieces and fragments" of a radical feminist text on women in culture and history,[18] including a completed draft of a chapter on the pornographic counterculture magazine *Suck*, which was published by a group of fellow expatriates in the Netherlands.[19]

Dworkin later wrote that she eventually agreed to help smuggle a briefcase of heroin through customs in return for $1,000 and an airplane ticket, thinking that if she was successful she could return home with the ticket and the money, and if caught she would at least escape her ex-husband's abuse by going to prison. The deal for the briefcase fell through, but the man who had promised Dworkin the money gave her the airline ticket anyway, and she returned to the United States in 1972.[20]

Before she left Amsterdam, Dworkin spoke with Abrams about her experiences in the Netherlands, the emerging feminist movement, and the book they had begun to write together. Dworkin agreed to complete the book — which she eventually titled *Woman Hating* — and publish it when she reached the United States.[21] In her memoirs, Dworkin relates that during that conversation she vowed to dedicate her life to the feminist movement:

> Sitting with Ricki, talking with Ricki, I made a vow to her: that I would use everything I knew, including from prostitution, to make the women's movement stronger and better; that I'd give my life to the movement and for the movement. I promised to be honor-bound to the well-being of women, to do anything necessary for that well-being. I promised to live and to die if need be for women. I made that vow some thirty years ago, and I have not betrayed it yet.
>
> — Andrea Dworkin, *Heartbreak: The Political Memoir of a Feminist Militant, 122.*

Return to New York and contact with the feminist movement

In New York, Dworkin worked again as an anti-war organizer, participated in demonstrations for lesbian rights and against apartheid in South Africa.[22] The feminist poet Muriel Rukeyser hired her as an assistant (Dworkin later said "I was the worst assistant in the history of the world. But Muriel kept me on because she believed in me as a writer."[23]) Dworkin also joined a feminist consciousness raising group,[24] and soon became involved in radical feminist organizing, focusing on campaigns against violence against women. In addition to her writing and activism, Dworkin gained notoriety as a speaker, mostly for events organized by local feminist groups.[25] She became well-known for passionate, uncompromising speeches that aroused strong feelings in both supporters and critics, and inspired her audience to action, such as her speech at the first Take Back the Night march in November 1978, and her 1983 speech at the Midwest Regional Conference of the National Organization for Changing Men (now the National Organization for Men Against Sexism[26]) entitled "I Want a Twenty-Four Hour Truce During Which There Is No Rape."[27]

Relationship with John Stoltenberg

In 1974, she met feminist writer and activist John Stoltenberg when they both walked out on a poetry reading in Greenwich Village over misogynist material. They became close friends and eventually came to live together.[28] Stoltenberg wrote a series of radical feminist books and articles on masculinity. Although Dworkin publicly wrote "I love John with my heart and soul"[29] and Stoltenberg described Dworkin as "the love of my life",[30] she continued to publicly identify herself as lesbian, and he as gay. Stoltenberg, recounting the perplexity that their relationship seemed to cause people in the press, summarized the relationship by saying "So I state only the simplest facts publicly: yes, Andrea and I live together and love each other and we are each other's life partner, and yes we are both out."[28]

Dworkin and Stoltenberg were married in 1998; after her death, Stoltenberg said "It's why we never told anybody really that we married, because people get confused about that. They think, Oh, she's yours. And we just did not want that nonsense."[30]

Critique of pornography

Andrea Dworkin is most often remembered for her role as a speaker, writer, and activist in the feminist anti-pornography movement.[31][32][33] In February 1976, Dworkin took a leading role in organizing public pickets of *Snuff* in New York City and, during the fall, joined Adrienne Rich, Grace Paley, Gloria Steinem, Shere Hite, Lois Gould, Barbara Deming, Karla Jay, Letty Cottin Pogrebin, Robin Morgan, and Susan Brownmiller in attempts to form a radical feminist antipornography group.[34] Members of this group would go on to found Women Against Pornography in 1979, but by then Dworkin had begun to distance herself from the group over differences in approach.[35] Dworkin spoke at the first Take Back the Night march in November 1978, and joined 3,000 women in a march through the red-light district of San Francisco.[36]

In 1979, Dworkin published *Pornography: Men Possessing Women*, which analyzes (and extensively cites examples drawn from) contemporary and historical pornography as an industry of woman-hating dehumanization. Dworkin argues that it is implicated in violence against women, both in its production (through the abuse of the women used to star in it), and in the social consequences of its consumption by encouraging men to eroticize the domination, humiliation, and abuse of women.[31][32][33]

Antipornography civil rights ordinance

In 1980, Linda Boreman (who had appeared in the pornographic film *Deep Throat* as "Linda Lovelace") made public statements that her ex-husband Chuck Traynor had beaten and raped her, and violently coerced her into making that and other pornographic films. Boreman made her charges public for the press corps at a press conference, with Dworkin, feminist lawyer Catharine MacKinnon, and members of Women Against Pornography. After the press conference, Dworkin, MacKinnon, Gloria Steinem, and Boreman began discussing the possibility of using federal civil rights law to seek damages from Traynor and the makers of *Deep Throat*. Boreman was interested, but backed off after Steinem discovered that the statute of limitations for a possible suit had passed.[37]

Dworkin and MacKinnon, however, continued to discuss civil rights litigation as a possible approach to combating pornography. In the fall of 1983, MacKinnon secured a one-semester appointment for Dworkin at the University of Minnesota, to teach a course in literature for the Women's Studies program and co-teach (with MacKinnon) an interdepartmental course on pornography, where they hashed out details of a civil rights approach. With encouragement from community activists in south Minneapolis, the Minneapolis city government hired Dworkin and MacKinnon to draft an antipornography civil rights ordinance as an amendment to the Minneapolis city civil rights ordinance. The amendment defined pornography as a civil rights violation against women, and allowed women who claimed harm from pornography to sue the producers and distributors in civil court for damages. The law was passed twice by the Minneapolis city council but vetoed by Mayor Don Fraser, who considered the wording of the ordinance to be too vague.[38] Another version of the ordinance passed in Indianapolis, Indiana in 1984, but overturned as unconstitutional by the Seventh Circuit Court of Appeals in the case *American Booksellers v. Hudnut*. Dworkin continued to support the civil rights approach in her writing and activism, and supported anti-pornography feminists who organized later campaigns in Cambridge, Massachusetts (1985) and Bellingham, Washington (1988) to pass versions of the ordinance by voter initiative.[39]

Right-Wing Women

In 1983, Dworkin published *Right-Wing Women: The Politics of Domesticated Females*, an examination of what she claimed were women's reasons for collaborating with men for the limitation of women's freedom.[40] In the Preface to the British edition,[41] Dworkin stated that the New Right in the United States focused especially on preserving male authority in the family, the promotion of fundamentalist versions of orthodox religion, combating abortion, and undermining efforts to combat domestic violence,[42] but that it also had, for the first time, "succeeded in getting *women as women* (women who claim to be acting in the interests of women as a group) to act effectively on behalf of male authority over women, on behalf of a hierarchy in which women are subservient to men, on behalf of women as the rightful property of men, on behalf of religion as an expression of transcendent male supremacy".[43] Taking this as her problem, Dworkin asked, "Why do right-wing women agitate for their own subordination? How does the Right, controlled by men, enlist their participation and loyalty? And why do right-wing women truly hate the feminist struggle for equality?"[44]

Testimony before Attorney General's Commission on Pornography

On January 22, 1986, Dworkin testified for half an hour before the Attorney General's Commission on Pornography (sometimes referred to as the "Meese Commission") in New York City, and answered questions from commissioners after completing her testimony.[45] Dworkin's testimony against pornography was praised and reprinted in the Commission's final report,[46] and Dworkin and MacKinnon marked its release by holding a joint press conference.[47] Meese Commission subsequently successfully demanded that convenience store chains remove from shelves men's magazines such as *Playboy*[47] (Dworkin wrote that the magazine "in both text and pictures promotes both rape and child sexual abuse")[48] and *Penthouse*.[49] The demands spread nationally and intimidated some retailers into withdrawing photography magazines, among others.[50] The Meese Commission's campaign was eventually quashed with a First Amendment admonishment against prior restraint by the D.C. Federal Court in Meese v. Playboy (639 F.Supp. 581).

In her testimony and replies to questions from the commissioners, Dworkin denounced the use of criminal obscenity prosecutions against pornographers, stating, "We are against obscenity laws. We do not want them. I want you to understand why, whether you end up agreeing or not."[51] She argued that obscenity laws were largely ineffectual,[51] that when they were effectual they only suppressed pornography from public view while allowing it to flourish out of sight,[52] and that they suppressed the wrong material, or the right material for the wrong reasons, arguing that "Obscenity laws are also woman-hating in their very construction. Their basic presumption is that it's women's bodies that are dirty."[53] Instead she offered five recommendations for the Commission, recommending (1) that "the Justice Department instruct law-enforcement agencies to keep records of the use of pornography in violent crimes",[53] (2) a ban on the possession and distribution of pornography in prisons,[54] (3) that prosecutors "enforce laws against pimping and pandering against pornographers",[54] (4) that the administration "make it a Justice Department priority to enforce RICO (the Racketeer Influenced and Corrupt Organizations Act) against the pornography industry",[54] and (5) that Congress adopt federal anti-pornography civil rights legislation which would provide for civil damages for harm inflicted on women. She suggested that the Commission consider "creating a criminal conspiracy provision under the civil rights law, such that conspiring to deprive a person of their civil rights by coercing them into pornography is a crime, and that conspiring to traffic in pornography is conspiring to deprive women of our civil rights".[55] Dworkin compared her proposal to the Southern Poverty Law Center's use of civil rights litigation against the Ku Klux Klan.[51]

Dworkin also submitted into evidence a copy of Boreman's book *Ordeal*, as an example of the abuses that she hoped to remedy, saying "The only thing atypical about Linda is that she has had the courage to make a public fight against what has happened to her. And whatever you come up with, it has to help her or it's not going to help anyone." Boreman had testified in person before the Commission, but the Commissioners had not yet seen her book.[56]

Intercourse

In 1987, Dworkin published *Intercourse*, in which she extended her analysis from pornography to sexual intercourse itself, and argued that the sort of sexual subordination depicted in pornography was central to men's and women's experiences of heterosexual intercourse in a male supremacist society. In the book, she argues that all heterosexual sex in our patriarchal society is coercive and degrading to women, and sexual penetration may by its very nature doom women to inferiority and submission, and "may be immune to reform."[57]

Citing from both pornography and literature—including *The Kreutzer Sonata*, *Madame Bovary*, and *Dracula*—Dworkin argued that depictions of intercourse in mainstream art and culture consistently emphasized heterosexual intercourse as the only kind of "real" sex, portrayed intercourse in violent or invasive terms, portrayed the violence or invasiveness as central to its eroticism, and often united it with male contempt for, revulsion towards, or even murder of, the "carnal" woman. She argued that this kind of depiction enforced a male-centric and coercive view of sexuality, and that, when the cultural attitudes combine with the material conditions of women's lives in a sexist society, the experience of heterosexual intercourse itself becomes a central part of men's subordination of women, experienced as a form of "occupation" that is nevertheless expected to be pleasurable for women and to define their very status *as women*.[58]

Such descriptions are often cited by Dworkin's critics, interpreting the book as claiming "all" heterosexual intercourse is rape, or more generally that the anatomical machinations of sexual intercourse make it intrinsically harmful to women's equality. For instance, Cathy Young[59] says that statements such as, "Intercourse is the pure, sterile, formal expression of men's contempt for women,"[57] are reasonably summarized as "All sex is rape."

Dworkin rejected that interpretation of her argument,[60] stating in a later interview that "I think both intercourse and sexual pleasure can and will survive equality"[61] and suggesting that the misunderstanding came about because of the very sexual ideology she was criticizing: "Since the paradigm for sex has been one of conquest, possession, and violation, I think many men believe they need an unfair advantage, which at its extreme would be called rape. I do not think they need it."[61]

Butler decision in Canada

In 1992, the Supreme Court of Canada made a ruling in *R. v. Butler* which incorporated some elements of Dworkin and MacKinnon's legal work on pornography into the existing Canadian obscenity law. In *Butler* the Court held that Canadian obscenity law violated Canadian citizens' rights to free speech under the Canadian Charter of Rights and Freedoms if enforced on grounds of morality or community standards of decency; but that obscenity law could be enforced constitutionally against some pornography on the basis of the Charter's guarantees of sex equality.[62] The Court's decision cited extensively from briefs prepared by the Women's Legal Education and Action Fund (LEAF), with the support and participation of Catharine MacKinnon.[63] Andrea Dworkin opposed LEAF's position, arguing that feminists should not support or attempt to reform criminal obscenity law.[64] In 1993, copies of Dworkin's book *Pornography* were held for inspection by Canada Customs agents,[65] fostering an urban legend that Dworkin's own books had been banned from Canada under a law that she herself had promoted. However, the *Butler* decision did not adopt Dworkin and MacKinnon's ordinance; Dworkin did not support the decision; and her books (which were released shortly after they were inspected) were held temporarily as part of a standard procedural measure, unrelated to the *Butler* decision.[66]

Fiction

Dworkin published three fictional works after achieving notability as a feminist author and activist. She published a collection of short stories, *The New Woman's Broken Heart* in 1980. Her first published novel, *Ice and Fire*, was published in the United Kingdom in 1986. It is a first-person narrative, rife with violence and abuse; Susie Bright has claimed that it amounts to a modern feminist rewriting of one of the Marquis de Sade's most famous works, *Juliette*.[67] However, Dworkin aimed to depict men's harm to women as normalized political harm, not as eccentric eroticism. Dworkin's second novel, *Mercy*, was published in the United Kingdom in 1990.

Dworkin's short fiction and novels often incorporated elements from her life and themes from her nonfiction writing, sometimes related by a first-person narrator. Critics have sometimes quoted passages spoken by characters in *Ice and Fire* as representations of Dworkin's own views.[68][69] cf.[60] Dworkin, however, wrote "My fiction is not autobiography. I am not an exhibitionist. I do not show myself. I am not asking for forgiveness. I do not want to confess. But I have used everything I know − my life − to show what I believe must be shown so that it can be faced. The imperative at the heart of my writing − what must be done − comes directly from my life. But I do not show my life directly, in full view; nor even look at it while others watch."[70]

Life and Death

In 1997, Dworkin published a collection of her speeches and articles from the 1990s in *Life and Death: Unapologetic Writings on the Continuing War on Women*, including a long autobiographical essay on her life as a writer, and articles on violence against women, pornography, prostitution, Nicole Brown Simpson, the use of rape during the war in Bosnia and Herzegovina, the Montreal massacre, Israel, and the gender politics of the United States Holocaust Memorial Museum.[71]

Reviewing *Life and Death* in *The New Republic*, philosopher Martha Nussbaum criticizes voices in contemporary feminism for denouncing Catharine MacKinnon and Dworkin as "man-haters," and argues that First Amendment critiques of Dworkin's civil ordinance proposal against pornography "are not saying anything intellectually respectable," for the First Amendment "has never covered all speech: bribery, threats, extortionate offers, misleading advertising, perjury, and unlicensed medical advice are all unprotected." Nussbaum adds that Dworkin has focused attention on the proper moral target by making harm associated with subordination, not obscenity, civilly actionable. Nevertheless, Nussbaum opposes the adoption of Dworkin's pornography ordinance because it (1) fails to distinguish between moral and legal violations, (2) fails to demonstrate a causal relationship between pornography and specific harm, (3) holds author of printed images or words responsible for others' behavior, (4) grants censorial power to the judiciary (which may be directed against feminist scholarship), and (5) erases the contextual considerations within which sex takes place. More broadly, Nussbaum faults for Dworkin for (1) occluding economic injustice through an "obsessive focus on sexual subordination," (2) reproducing objectification in reducing her interlocutors to their abuse, and (3) refusing reconciliation in favor of "violent extralegal resistance against male violence."[72]

Later life

In the same year, the *New York Times Book Review* published a lengthy letter of hers in which she describes the origins of her deeply felt hatred of prostitution and pornography ("mass-produced, technologized prostitution") as her history of being violently inspected by prison doctors, battered by her first husband and numerous other men.[73]

Unlike most feminist leaders , Dworkin was a strong opponent of President Bill Clinton during the Lewinsky scandal.[74] She also expressed support for Paula Jones and Juanita Broaddrick.[75]

In 2000, she published *Scapegoat: The Jews, Israel, and Women's Liberation*, in which she compared the oppression of women to the persecution of Jews,[60] discussed the sexual politics of Jewish identity and anti-Semitism, and called for the establishment of a women's homeland as a response to the oppression of women.[76][77][78]

In June 2000, Dworkin published controversial articles in the *New Statesman*[79] and in the *Guardian*,[80] stating that one or more men had raped her in her hotel room in Paris the previous year, putting GHB in her drink to disable her. Her articles ignited public controversy[81] when writers such as Catherine Bennett[82] and Julia Gracen[83] published doubts about her account, polarizing opinion between skeptics and supporters such as Catharine MacKinnon, Katharine Viner,[32] and Gloria Steinem. Her reference to the incident was later described by Charlotte Raven as a "widely disbelieved claim," better seen as "a kind of artistic housekeeping."[84] Emotionally fragile and in failing health, Dworkin mostly withdrew from public life for two years following the articles.[28][31][79][80][82][83][85][86][87]

In 2002, Dworkin published her autobiography, *Heartbreak: The Political Memoir of a Feminist Militant*. She soon began to speak and write again, and in interview with Julie Bindel in 2004 said, "I thought I was finished, but I feel a new vitality. I want to continue to help women."[31] She published three more articles in the *Guardian* and began work on a new book, *Writing America: How Novelists Invented and Gendered a Nation*, on the role of novelists such as Ernest Hemingway and William Faulkner in the development of American political and cultural identity, which was left unfinished when she died.[71]

Illness and death

During her final years, Dworkin suffered fragile health, and she revealed in her last column for the *Guardian* that she had been weakened and nearly crippled for the past several years by severe osteoarthritis in the knees.[88] Shortly after returning from Paris in 1999, she had been hospitalized with a high fever and blood clots in her legs. A few months after being released from the hospital, she became increasingly unable to bend her knees, and underwent surgery to replace her knees with titanium and plastic prosthetics. She wrote, "The doctor who knows me best says that osteoarthritis begins long before it cripples—in my case, possibly from homelessness, or sexual abuse, or beatings on my legs, or my weight. John, my partner, blames *Scapegoat*, a study of Jewish identity and women's liberation that took me nine years to write; it is, he says, the book that stole my health. I blame the drug-rape that I experienced in 1999 in Paris."[88]

When a newspaper interviewer asked her how she would like to be remembered, she said "In a museum, when male supremacy is dead. I'd like my work to be an anthropological artifact from an extinct, primitive society."[33] She died in her sleep on the morning of April 9, 2005, at her home in Washington, D.C.[89] The cause of death was later determined to be acute myocarditis.[90] She was 58 years old.

Legacy and controversy

Dworkin authored ten books of radical feminist theory and numerous speeches and articles, each designed to assert the presence of and denounce institutionalized and normalized harm against women. She became one of the most influential writers and spokeswomen of American radical feminism during the late 1970s and the 1980s.[32][85] She characterized pornography as an industry of damaging objectification and abuse, not merely a fantasy realm. She discussed prostitution as a system of exploitation, and intercourse as a key site of subordination in patriarchy. Her analysis and writing influenced and inspired the work of contemporary feminists, such as Catharine MacKinnon,[91] Gloria Steinem,[92] John Stoltenberg,[89] Nikki Craft,[93] Susan Cole,[94] and Amy Elman.[95]

Dworkin's uncompromising positions and forceful style of writing and speaking, described by Robert Campbell as "apocalyptic,"[96] earned her frequent comparisons to other speakers such as Malcolm X (by Robin Morgan,[89] Susie Bright,[67] and others). Gloria Steinem repeatedly compared her style to that of the Old Testament prophets;[97][98] Susan Brownmiller recalls her Take Back the Night speech in 1978:

> Saturday evening culminated in a candlelit "Take Back the Night" march (the first of its kind) through the porn district, kicked off by an exhortation by Andrea Dworkin. I'd seen Andrea in my living room, but this was the first time I'd seen Andrea in action. On the spot I dubbed her Rolling Thunder. Perspiring in her trademark denim coveralls, she employed the rhetorical cadences that would make her both a cult idol and an object of ridicule a few years later. Dworkin's dramatized martyrdom and revival-tent theatrics never sat well with me, but I retained my respect for her courage long after I absented myself from the pornography wars. Her call to action accomplished, three thousand demonstrators took to the streets ...
>
> — Susan Brownmiller, **'In Our Time: Memoir of a Revolution,** *302–303*

Many of Dworkin's early speeches are reprinted in her second book, *Our Blood* (1976). Later selections of speeches were reprinted ten and twenty years later, in *Letters from a War Zone* (1988) and *Life and Death* (1997).[71]

She maintained some political communication with the political right wing. She authored the book *Right-Wing Women*, reviewed as premised on agreement between feminists and right-wing women on the existence of domination by men in sex and class and disagreement on strategy.[99] She testified at a Meese Commission hearing on pornography, while Attorney General Edwin Meese was serving socially conservative President Reagan. She had a political discourse with *National Review* writer David Frum and their spouses arranged by Christopher Hitchens;[100][101] the *National Review* is a U.S. conservative political movement magazine.

Her attitude and language often sharply polarized debate, and made Dworkin herself a figure of intense controversy. After her death, the conservative gay writer Andrew Sullivan claimed that "Many on the social right liked Andrea Dworkin. Like Dworkin, their essential impulse when they see human beings living freely is to try and control or stop them — for their own good. Like Dworkin, they are horrified by male sexuality, and see men as such as a problem to be tamed. Like Dworkin, they believe in the power of the state to censor and coerce sexual freedoms. Like Dworkin, they view the enormous new freedom that women and gay people have acquired since the 1960s as a terrible development for human culture."[102] Libertarian/conservative[103] journalist Cathy Young complained of a "whitewash" in feminist obituaries for Dworkin, argued that Dworkin's positions were manifestly misandrist, stated that Dworkin was in fact insane,[104][105] criticized what she called Dworkin's "destructive legacy", and described Dworkin as a "sad ghost" that feminism needs to exorcise.[106]

Other feminists, however, published sympathetic or celebratory memorials online and in print.[107][108] Catharine MacKinnon, Dworkin's longtime friend and collaborator, published a column in the *New York Times*, celebrating what she described as Dworkin's "incandescent literary and political career," suggested that Dworkin deserved a nomination for the Nobel Prize in Literature, and complained that "Lies about her views on sexuality (that she believed intercourse was rape) and her political alliances (that she was in bed with the right) were published and republished without attempts at verification, corrective letters almost always refused. Where the physical appearance of male writers is regarded as irrelevant or cherished as a charming eccentricity, Andrea's was reviled and mocked and turned into pornography. When she sued for libel, courts trivialized the pornographic lies as fantasy and dignified them as satire."[107]

Dworkin's reports of violence suffered at the hands of men sometimes aroused skepticism, the most famous example being the public controversy over her allegations of being drugged and raped in Paris. In 1989, Dworkin wrote an article about her life as a battered wife in the Netherlands, "What Battery Really Is," in response to fellow radical feminist Susan Brownmiller, who had argued that Hedda Nussbaum, a battered woman, should have been indicted for her failure to stop Joel Steinberg from murdering their adoptive daughter. *Newsweek* initially accepted "What Battery Really Is" for publication, but then declined to publish the account at the request of their attorney, according to Dworkin, arguing that she needed either to publish anonymously "to protect the identity of the batterer" and remove references to specific injuries, or to provide "medical records, police records, a written statement from a doctor who had seen the injuries." Instead, Dworkin submitted the article to the *Los Angeles Times*, which published it on March 12, 1989.[109]

Some critics, such as Larry Flynt's magazine *Hustler*[110] and Gene Healy,[111] allege that Dworkin endorsed incest. In the closing chapter of *Woman Hating* (1974), Dworkin wrote that "The parent-child relationship is primarily erotic because all human relationships are primarily erotic," and that "The incest taboo, because it denies us essential fulfillment with the parents whom we love with our primary energy, forces us to internalize those parents and constantly seek them. The incest taboo does the worst work of the culture ... The destruction of the incest taboo is essential to the development of cooperative human community based on the free-flow of natural androgynous eroticism."[112] Dworkin, however, does not explain if "fulfillment" is supposed to involve actual sexual intimacy, and one page earlier characterized what she meant by "erotic relationships" as relationships whose "substance is nonverbal communication and touch,"[113] which she explicitly distinguished from what she referred to as "fucking."[114]

Dworkin's work from the early 1980s onward contained frequent condemnations of incest and pedophilia as one of the chief forms of violence against women, arguing that "Incest is terrifically important in understanding the condition of women. It is a crime committed against someone, a crime from which many victims never recover."[115][116] In the early 1980s she had a public row with her former friend Allen Ginsberg over his support for child pornography and pedophilia, in which Ginsberg said "The right wants to put me in jail," and Dworkin responded "Yes, they're very sentimental; I'd kill you."[117] When *Hustler* published the claim that Dworkin advocated incest in 1985, Dworkin sued them for defamatory libel; the court dismissed Dworkin's complaint on the grounds that whether the allegations were true or false, a faulty interpretation of a work placed into the "marketplace of ideas" did not amount to defamation in the legal sense.[110]

Other critics, especially women who identify as feminists but sharply differ with Dworkin's style or positions, have offered nuanced views, suggesting that Dworkin called attention to real and important problems, but that her legacy as a whole had been destructive to the women's movement.[118] Her work and activism on pornography—especially in the form of the Antipornography Civil Rights Ordinance—drew heavy criticism from groups such as the Feminist Anti-Censorship Task Force (FACT). Dworkin also attracted criticism from sex-positive feminists, who emerged largely in opposition to the feminist anti-pornography movement during the 1980s, as Dworkin was becoming prominent on the national stage. Sex-positive feminist critics criticized her legal activism as censorious, and argued that her work on pornography and sexuality promoted an essentialist, conservative, or repressive view of sexuality, which they often characterized as "anti-sex" or "sex-negative." Her criticisms of common heterosexual sexual expression, pornography, prostitution, and sexual sadism were frequently claimed to disregard women's own agency in sex or to deny women's sexual choices. Dworkin countered that her critics often misrepresented her views,[119] and that under the heading of "choice" and "sex-positivity" her feminist critics were failing to question the often violent political structures that confined women's choices and shaped the meaning of sex acts.[120]

Publications

In addition to books, articles, and speeches listed here, she wrote for anthologies and wrote additional articles, and some of her works were translated into other languages.[121]

Nonfiction

- *Heartbreak: The Political Memoir of a Feminist Militant* (2002) ISBN 0-465-01754-1
- *Scapegoat: The Jews, Israel, and Women's Liberation* (2000) ISBN 0-684-83612-2
- *Life and Death: Unapologetic Writings on the Continuing War Against Women* (1997) ISBN 0-684-83512-6
- *In Harm's Way: The Pornography Civil Rights Hearings* (with Catharine MacKinnon, 1997) ISBN 0-674-44579-1
- *Letters from a War Zone: Writings* (1988) ISBN 1-55652-185-5 ISBN 0-525-24824-2 ISBN 0-436-13962-6
- *Pornography and Civil Rights: A New Day for Women's Equality* (1988) ISBN 0-9621849-0-X
- *Intercourse* (1987) ISBN 0-684-83239-9
- *Right-Wing Women: The Politics of Domesticated Females* (1983) ISBN 0-399-50671-3
- *Pornography—Men Possessing Women* (1981) ISBN 0-399-50532-6 — Online summary [122], excerpts [123]
- *Our Blood: Prophesies and Discourses on Sexual Politics* (1976) ISBN 0-399-50575-X ISBN 0-06-011116-X
- *Woman Hating: A Radical Look at Sexuality* (Dutton, 1974) ISBN 0-452-26827-3 ISBN 0-525-48397-7

Fiction and poetry

- *Mercy* (1990, ISBN 0-941423-88-3)
- *Ice and Fire* (1986, ISBN 0-436-13960-X)
- *The New Woman's Broken Heart: Short Stories* (1980, ISBN 0-9603628-0-0)
- *Morning Hair* (self-published, 1968)
- *Child* (1966) (Heraklion, Crete, 1966)

Articles

- Marx and Gandhi were liberals: Feminism and the "radical" left (1977 (ASIN B0006XEJCG))
- Why so-called radical men love and need pornography (1978 (ASIN B0006XX57G))
- Against the male flood: Censorship, pornography and equality (1985 (ASIN B00073AVJA))
- The reasons why: Essays on the new civil rights law recognizing pornography as sex discrimination (1985 (ASIN B000711OSO))
- Pornography is a civil rights issue for women (1986 (ASIN B00071HFYG))
- A good rape. (1996 (ASIN B0008DT8DE)) (Book Review)
- Out of the closet.(Normal: Transsexual CEOs, Cross-Dressing Cops and Hermaphrodites with Attitude) (1996 (ASIN B0008E679Q)) (Book Review)
- The day I was drugged and raped (1996 (ASIN B0008IYNJS))
- Are you listening, Hillary? President Rape is who he is (1999) (excerpt)[124]

Speeches and interviews

Some were digitalized.

- Why Men Like Pornography & Prostitution So Much [125] Andrea Dworkin Keynote Speech at International Trafficking Conference, 1989. *(Audio File: 22 min, 128 kbit/s, mp3)*
- Andrea Dworkin's Attorney General's Commission Testimony [126] on Pornography and Prostitution
- Violence, Abuse & Women's Citizenship Brighton [127], UK November 10, 1996
- "Freedom Now: Ending Violence Against Women" [128]
- "Speech from Duke University, January, 1985" [129]
- Taped Phone Interview [130] Andrea Dworkin interviewed by Nikki Craft on Allen Ginsberg, May 9, 1990. (Audio File, 20 min, 128 kbit/s, mp3)
- *Dworkin on Dworkin, ca. 1980*[131]

Reviews of Dworkin's works

- *Ice and Fire*, by Andrea Dworkin; *Intercourse*, by Andrea Dworkin. "Male and Female, Men and Women" [132]. Reviewed by Carol Sternhell for the *New York Times* (May 3, 1987).
- *Intercourse*, by Andrea Dworkin; *Feminism Unmodified*, by Catharine MacKinnon. "Porn in the U.S.A., Part I" [133]. Reviewed by Maureen Mullarkey for *The Nation* (May 30, 1987):
- *Intercourse*, by Andrea Dworkin (Tenth Anniversary Edition 1997) [134]. Reviewed by Giney Villar for *Women in Action* (3:1998).
- *Pornography: Men Possessing Women*. "Unburning a Witch: Re-Reading Andrea Dworkin" [135]. Reviewed by Jed Brandt for the *NYC Indypendent* (February 7, 2005).

Related work

She was a member of The American Heritage Dictionary's Usage Panel.[136]

References

[1] http://www.andreadworkin.com/
[2] Dworkin, *Heartbreak*, p. 23.
[3] Dworkin, *Life and Death*, p. 3.
[4] Dworkin, *Heartbreak*, pp. 21–22.
[5] Dworkin, *Life and Death*, pp. 23–24, 28; Dworkin, *Heartbreak*, pp. 37–40.
[6] *Dworkin, Andrea. Videotape Collection of Andrea Dworkin, 1981–1998 (Inclusive): A Finding Aid* (Cambridge, Mass.: Arthur and Elizabeth Schlesinger Library on the History of Women in America, Radcliffe Institute for Advanced Study, Harvard Univ. (Vt-136), Feb., 2009) (http://oasis.lib.harvard.edu/oasis/deliver/~sch01210), as accessed Jul. 31, 2011.
[7] Dworkin, *Heartbreak*, pp. 77-81.
[8] Dworkin, *Heartbreak*, p. 80.
[9] Dworkin, *Heartbreak*, pp. 80, 83.
[10] Dworkin, *Heartbreak*, pp. 83–85, 87.

[11] Dworkin, *Heartbreak*, p. 98.

[12] Dworkin, *Heartbreak*, pp. 107–112.

[13] Dworkin, *Life and Death*, pp. 24–25; Dworkin, *Heartbreak*, p. 117.

[14] Dworkin, *Heartbreak*, p. 119; Dworkin, *Letters from a War Zone*, pp. 103, 332.

[15] Dworkin, *Life and Death*, p. 17.

[16] Dworkin, *Life and Death*, 18–19

[17] Dworkin, *Life and Death*, p. 19; Dworkin, *Heartbreak*, p. 118.

[18] Dworkin, *Woman Hating*, Acknowledgment, p. 7.

[19] Dworkin, *Life and Death*, p. 21; Dworkin, *Heartbreak*, p. 122.

[20] Dworkin, *Letters from a War Zone*, pp. 332–333; Dworkin, *Life and Death*, p. 22.

[21] Dworkin, *Life and Death*, p. 22.

[22] Dworkin, *Heartbreak*, p. 123.

[23] Dworkin, *Letters from a War Zone*, p. 3.

[24] Dworkin, *Heartbreak*, p. 124.

[25] Dworkin, *Heartbreak*, pp. 139–143.

[26] "A Brief History of NOMAS" (http://www.nomas.org/history). National Organization for Men Against Sexism. . Retrieved July 5, 2009.

[27] Dworkin (Fall 1983). "I Want a Twenty-Four Hour Truce During Which There Is No Rape" (http://www.nostatusquo.com/ACLU/dworkin/WarZoneChaptIIIE.html). *Letters from a War Zone*. pp. 162–171. . Retrieved July 5, 2009.

[28] John Stoltenberg (May/June 1994). "Living with Andrea Dworkin" (http://www.nostatusquo.com/ACLU/dworkin/LivingWithAndrea.html). *Lambda Book Report*. . Retrieved July 5, 2009.

[29] Dworkin (1994). "Andrea Dworkin" (http://www.nostatusquo.com/ACLU/dworkin/AutobiographyIII.html). *Contemporary Authors Autobiography Series, Vol. 21*. Farmington Hills, Mich.: Thomson Gale. ISBN 0810345188. . Retrieved July 5, 2009.

[30] John Stoltenberg (April 30, 2005). "Imagining Life Without Andrea" (http://www.feminist.com/resources/artspeech/genwom/andreadworkin.html). Feminist.com. . Retrieved July 5, 2009.

[31] Julie Bindel (September 30, 2004). "A life without compromise" (http://www.guardian.co.uk/books/2004/sep/30/gender.world). *The Guardian* (London). . Retrieved July 11, 2009.

[32] Katharine Viner (April 12, 2005). "'She never hated men'" (http://www.guardian.co.uk/books/2005/apr/12/gender.highereducation). *The Guardian* (London). . Retrieved July 11, 2009.

[33] Julie Bindel (April 12, 2005). "Obituary" (http://www.guardian.co.uk/news/2005/apr/12/guardianobituaries.gender). *The Guardian* (London). . Retrieved July 12, 2009.

[34] Susan Brownmiller (1999). *In Our Time: Memoir of a Revolution*. New York: Dial Press. pp. 297–299. ISBN 0385314868.

[35] Brownmiller, *In Our Time*, pp. 303, 316.

[36] Brownmiller, *In Our Time*, pp. 391–392.

[37] Brownmiller, *In Our Time*, p. 337.

[38] Donald Alexander Downs (1989). "The Minneapolis Ordinance and the Feminist Theory of Pornography and Sexuality" (http://books.google.com/books?id=4h4rpVBqtMgC&pg=PA34). *The New Politics of Pornography*. Chicago: University of Chicago Press. pp. 34–65. ISBN 0-226-16162-5. .

[39] Dworkin, *Life and Death*, pp. 90–95.

[40] Dworkin (1983). "Abortion" (http://www.nostatusquo.com/ACLU/dworkin/RightWingWomenAbortion.html). *Right Wing Women*. . Retrieved July 8, 2009.

[41] Reprinted in Dworkin, *Letters from a War Zone*, pp. 185–194.

[42] Dworkin, *Letters from a War Zone*, pp. 192–193.

[43] Dworkin, *Letters from a War Zone*, p. 193.

[44] Dworkin, *Letters from a War Zone*, p. 194.

[45] Dworkin's testimony, "Pornography Is a Civil Rights Issue", is reprinted in Dworkin, *Letters from a War Zone*, pp. 276–307.

[46] "Victimization" (http://www.porn-report.com/401-victimization.htm). *Attorney General's Commission on Pornography*. 1986. . Retrieved July 8, 2009.

[47] Pat Califia (1994). "The Obscene, Disgusting, and Vile Meese Commission Report" (http://cultronix.eserver.org/califia/meese/). *Public Sex: The Culture of Radical Sex*. San Francisco: Cleis Press. . Retrieved July 8, 2009.

[48] Colleen McEneany. "Pornography and Feminism" (http://web.archive.org/web/20060720195949/http://www.amazoncastle.com/feminism/porn.shtml). FeministUtopia. Archived from the original (http://www.amazoncastle.com/feminism/porn.shtml) on July 20, 2006. . Retrieved July 8, 2009.

[49] David M. Edwards. "Politics and Pornography: A Comparison of the Findings of the President's Commission and the Meese Commission and the Resulting Response" (http://home.earthlink.net/~durangodave/html/writing/Censorship.htm). . Retrieved July 9, 2009.

[50] Christopher M. Finan and Anne F. Castro. "The Rev. Donald E. Wildmon's Crusade for Censorship, 1977-1992" (http://www.mediacoalition.org/reports/wildmon.html). Media Coalition. . Retrieved July 9, 2009.

[51] Dworkin, *Letters from a War Zone*, p. 285.

[52] Dworkin, *Letters from a War Zone*, pp. 285–286.

[53] Dworkin, *Letters from a War Zone*, p. 286.

[54] Dworkin, *Letters from a War Zone*, p. 287.

[55] Dworkin, *Letters from a War Zone*, p. 288.

[56] Dworkin, *Letters from a War Zone*, p. 289.

[57] Dworkin. "Occupation/Collaboration" (http://faculty.uccb.ns.ca/sstewart/sexlove/dworkin.htm). *Intercourse*. . Retrieved July 8, 2009.

[58] Dworkin. "Occupation/Collaboration" (http://www.nostatusquo.com/ACLU/dworkin/IntercourseI.html). *Intercourse*. . Retrieved July 8, 2009.

[59] Cathy Young. "Woman's Hating: The misdirected passion of Andrea Dworkin" (http://reason.com/archives/2005/04/19/womans-hating). .

[60] Nikki Craft. "The Andrea Dworkin Lie Detector" (http://www.nostatusquo.com/ACLU/dworkin/LieDetect.html). Andrea Dworkin Online Library. . Retrieved July 8, 2009.

[61] Michael Moorcock (April 21, 1995). "Fighting Talk" (http://www.nostatusquo.com/ACLU/dworkin/MoorcockInterview.html). *New Statesman and Society*. . Retrieved July 8, 2009.

[62] Brenda Cossman (1997). "Feminist Fashion or Morality in Drag? The Sexual Subtext of the *Butler* Decision" (http://books.google.com/books?id=KfTtZl-hrBsC&pg=PA107). *Bad Attitude/s on Trial: Pornography, Feminism, and the* Butler *Decision*. Toronto: University of Toronto Press. p. 107. ISBN 0-8020-7643-2. .

[63] Christopher Jon Nowlin (2003). *Judging Obscenity: A Critical History of Expert Evidence* (http://books.google.com/books?id=spUwNzRGwLgC&pg=PA126). Quebec: McGill-Queen's University Press. p. 126. ISBN 0-7735-2538-6. .

[64] Joan Mason-Grant (2004). *Pornography Embodied: From Speech to Sexual Practice* (http://books.google.com/
      books?id=ZlGmGa8LMmgC&pg=PA176). Lanham, Md.: Rowman & Littlefield. p. 176, n. 30. ISBN 0-7425-1223-1. .

[65] Zachary Margulis (March 1995). "Canada's Thought Police" (http://www.wired.com/wired/archive/3.03/canada.html). *Wired*. .
      Retrieved July 8, 2009.

[66] Catharine A. MacKinnon and Andrea Dworkin (August 26, 1994). "Statement by Catharine A. MacKinnon and Andrea Dworkin Regarding
      Canadian Customs and Legal Approaches to Pornography" (http://www.nostatusquo.com/ACLU/dworkin/OrdinanceCanada.html). .
      Retrieved July 8, 2009.

[67] Susie Bright (April 11, 2005). "Andrea Dworkin Has Died" (http://susiebright.blogs.com/susie_brights_journal_/2005/04/
      andrea_dworkin_.html). . Retrieved July 11, 2009.

[68] Gladden Schrock. "Feminist Hate-Speech" (http://www.fatherhoodcoalition.org/cpf/newreadings/2001/feminist_hate_speech.htm).
      The Fatherhood Coalition. . Retrieved July 11, 2009.

[69] Eric Ross. "Mind-Programming of the Masses" (http://web.archive.org/web/20080508232955/http://www.mensnewsdaily.com/
      archive/r/ross-eric/2005/ross072205.htm). *MacDworkinism and VAWA: The Fraud of the Millennia*. Archived from the original (http://
      www.mensnewsdaily.com/archive/r/ross-eric/2005/ross072205.htm) on May 8, 2008. . Retrieved July 11, 2009.

[70] Dworkin, *Life and Death*, p. 15.

[71] "Obituary" (http://www.timesonline.co.uk/tol/comment/obituaries/article380289.ece). *The Times* (London). April 13, 2005. .
      Retrieved July 18, 2009.

[72] Nussbaum, Martha C. "Rage and Reason." *The New Republic*. August 11, 1997, pp. 36-42.

[73] Dworkin (May 3, 1992). "Pornography and the New Puritans" (http://www.nytimes.com/books/97/06/15/lifetimes/25885.html). *The
      New York Times*. . Retrieved July 11, 2009.

[74] James Taranto (August 4, 1998). "Who's a Hypocrite—and Who Cares?" (http://www.jamestaranto.com/hypo.htm). *The Wall Street
      Journal*. . Retrieved March 4, 2011.

[75] Candice E. Jackson. *Their Lives: The Women Targeted by the Clinton Machine*. Torrance, Calif.: World Ahead Publishing. p. 240.

[76] Dworkin, Andrea, *Scapegoat: The Jews, Israel, and Women's Liberation* (N.Y.: Free Press, 2000 (ISBN 0-684-83612-2)), pp. 246,
      245–246, 336, & 248.

[77] *Take No Prisoners*, in *The Guardian*, May 13, 2000 (http://www.guardian.co.uk/books/2000/may/13/politics1), as accessed Sep. 6,
      2010.

[78] Ouma, Veronica A., *Dworkin's Scapegoating*, in *Palestine Solidarity Review* (*PSR*), Fall 2005 (http://psreview.org/content/view/38/99/
      ), as accessed Oct. 21, 2010 (citing, in part, in *Scapegoat*, *id.*, pp. 336 & 337).

[79] Dworkin (June 5, 2000). "The day I was drugged and raped" (http://www.newstatesman.com/200006050009). *New Statesman*. .
      Retrieved July 11, 2009.

[80] Dworkin (June 2, 2000). "'They took my body from me and used it'" (http://www.guardian.co.uk/books/2000/jun/02/society). *The
      Guardian* (London). . Retrieved July 11, 2009.

[81] David A. Roberts (April 27, 2005). "A Post-Mortem Analysis of Andrea Dworkin" (http://www.ifeminists.net/introduction/editorials/
      2005/0427droberts.html). ifeminist.com. . Retrieved July 11, 2009.

[82] Catherine Bennett (June 8, 2000). "Doubts about Dworkin" (http://www.guardian.co.uk/books/2000/jun/08/society). *The Guardian*
      (London). . Retrieved July 11, 2009.

[83] Julia Gracen (September 20, 2000). "Andrea Dworkin in Agony" (http://archive.salon.com/books/feature/2000/09/20/dworkin/index.
      html). Salon.com. . Retrieved July 11, 2009.

[84] Charlotte Raven (June 19, 2006). "Body of Evidence" (http://www.newstatesman.com/200606190055). *New Statesman*. . Retrieved July
      11, 2009.

[85] Louise Armstrong (July 25, 2001). "The Trouble with Andrea" (http://www.guardian.co.uk/world/2001/jun/25/gender.uk1). *The
      Guardian* (London). . Retrieved July 11, 2009.

[86] Pat Califia, ed. *Forbidden Passages: Writings Banned in Canada*. Pittsburgh: Cleis Press, 1995.

[87] Adam Parfrey. "The Devil and Andrea Dworkin," in *Cult Rapture*. Portland, Ore.:Feral House Books, 1995. pp. 53–62.

[88] Dworkin (April 23, 2005). "Through the pain barrier" (http://www.guardian.co.uk/books/2005/apr/23/features.weekend). *The
      Guardian* (London). . Retrieved July 11, 2009.

[89] Ariel Levy (May 29, 2005). "The Prisoner of Sex" (http://nymag.com/nymetro/news/people/features/11907/). *New York*. . Retrieved
      July 12, 2009.

[90] Beth Ribet (March 11, 2006). "First Year: An Interview with John Stoltenberg" (http://www.andreadworkin.net/memorial/
      stoltinterview.html). . Retrieved July 12, 2009.

[91] Stuart Jeffries (April 12, 2006). "Are women human?" (http://www.guardian.co.uk/world/2006/apr/12/gender.
      politicsphilosophyandsociety). *The Guardian* (London). . Retrieved July 18, 2009.

[92] Zoe Heller (December 6, 1992). "The New Eve" (http://www.independent.co.uk/arts-entertainment/
      the-new-eve-these-are-some-common-perceptions-about-andrea-dworkin-that-she-hates-men-that-she-hates-sex-and-has-no-real-understanding-of-either-wro
      html). *The Independent* (London). . Retrieved July 18, 2009.

[93] Nikki Craft. "The Nikki Wiki: All About Nikki Craft" (http://www.nikkicraft.com/). . Retrieved July 18, 2009.

[94] Susan G. Cole (May 12–19, 2005). "Sex, lies and ideologies". *NOW*.

[95] Max Waltman (May 2009). "The Civil Rights and Equality Deficit: Legal Challenges to Pornography and Sex Inequality in Canada,
      Sweden, and the U.S." (http://www.cpsa-acsp.ca/papers-2009/Waltman.pdf) (PDF). Canadian Political Science Association. . Retrieved
      July 18, 2009.

[96] Robert L. Campbell (March 29, 2004). "Radical Feminism: Some Thoughts on Long's Defense" (http://hnn.us/blogs/entries/4351.html).
      History News Network. . Retrieved July 12, 2009.

[97] Mark Honigsbaum (April 12, 2005). "Andrea Dworkin, embattled feminist, dies at 58" (http://www.guardian.co.uk/world/2005/apr/
      12/obituaries.gender). *The Guardian* (London). . Retrieved July 12, 2009.

[98] "Gloria Steinem Remembers Feminist Writer and Activist Andrea Dworkin" (http://www.democracynow.org/2005/6/23/
      gloria_steinem_remembers_feminist_writer_and). *Democracy Now!*. March 29, 2004. . Retrieved July 12, 2009.

[99] Apparently untitled review, by Sallie L. Foster, in *Library Journal*, vol. 108, issue 1 (01/01/83) (ISSN 03630277), p. 59, [§] *Social Science*
      (book review), in *MasterFile Premier* (EbscoHost) (database) (PDF Full Text) (http://web.ebscohost.com/ehost/pdfviewer/
      pdfviewer?vid=5&hid=105&sid=6b125cef-4fd9-4b03-af76-1751a8dbe32b@sessionmgr114), as accessed May 21, 2010, reviewing
      Right-Wing Women: The Politics of Domesticated Females, by Andrea Dworkin, Jan. 1983 (ISBN 0-698-11171-0 or ISBN 0-399-50671-3
      (pap.)) (alternate link (http://web.ebscohost.com/ehost/detail?vid=4&hid=105&
      sid=6b125cef-4fd9-4b03-af76-1751a8dbe32b@sessionmgr114&bdata=JnNpdGU9ZWhvc3QtbGl2ZQ==#db=f5h&AN=7544468#db=f5h&
      AN=7544468#db=f5h&AN=7544468), as accessed the same day).

[100] *Andrea Dworkin RIP*, in *David Frum's Diary*, in *National Review Online*, § *NRO Blog Row*, Apr. 12, 2005 (http://frum.nationalreview.
      com/post/?q=YjA2MGNlZDc1NmNmYzY2NGQ0NjdkMGIzMWMwZDc1ZjM=), as accessed May 9, 2010.

[101] *The Nation: Seeing Eye to Eye; A Radical Feminist Who Could Dine With (Not On) Conservatives*, in *N.Y. Times*, § *Week In Review*, Apr. 17, 2005 (http://query.nytimes.com/gst/fullpage.html?res=9A02E0D6113EF934A25757C0A9639C8B63), as accessed May 9, 2010.

[102] Andrew Sullivan (April 18, 2005). "Daily Dish" (http://sullivanarchives.theatlantic.com/index.php.dish_inc-archives. 2005_04_01_dish_archive.html#111384129072050618). *The Atlantic.* . Retrieved July 5, 2009.

[103] Cathy Young. "Welcome to the website of writer and journalist Cathy Young" (http://www.cathyyoung.net/). . Retrieved July 12, 2009.

[104] Cathy Young (November 24, 2005). "Anti-feminist? *Moi*?" (http://cathyyoung.blogspot.com/2005/11/anti-feminist-moi.html). . Retrieved July 12, 2009.

[105] Cathy Young (April 17, 2005). "The Dworkin Whitewash" (http://www.reason.com/blog/show/109179.html). . Retrieved July 12, 2009.

[106] Cathy Young (April 18, 2005). "The Misdirected Passion of Andrea Dworkin" (http://www.boston.com/news/globe/editorial_opinion/ oped/articles/2005/04/18/the_misdirected_passion_of_andrea_dworkin/). *The Boston Globe.* . Retrieved July 12, 2009.

[107] MacKinnon, Catharine A. (April 16, 2005). "Who Was Afraid of Andrea Dworkin?" (http://www.nytimes.com/2005/04/16/opinion/ 16mackinnon.html). *The New York Times.* . Retrieved July 12, 2009.

[108] "Andrea Dworkin Dies" (http://web.archive.org/web/20061225074237/http://www.msmusings.net/archives/2005/04/ andrea_dworkin.html). *Ms.*. April 11, 2005. Archived from the original (http://www.msmusings.net/archives/2005/04/andrea_dworkin. html) on December 25, 2006. . Retrieved July 12, 2009.

[109] Dworkin, *Letters from a War Zone*, p. 330.

[110] "*Dworkin v. L.F.P., Inc.*, 1992 WY 120, 839 P.2d 903" (http://wyomcases.courts.state.wy.us/applications/oscn/DeliverDocument. asp?citeID=122816). . Retrieved July 12, 2009.

[111] Gene Healy (May/June 1998). "Andrea Dworkin: I Just Don't Get It" (http://web.archive.org/web/20061208203708/http://criterion. uchicago.edu/issues/ii6/healy.html). *Criterion*. Archived from the original (http://criterion.uchicago.edu/issues/ii6/healy.html) on December 8, 2006. . Retrieved July 18, 2009.

[112] Dworkin, *Woman Hating*, p. 189.

[113] Dworkin, *Woman Hating*, p. 188.

[114] Dworkin, *Woman Hating*, p. 187.

[115] Dworkin, *Letters from a War Zone*, pp. 139–142, 149, 176–180, 308, 314–315; Dworkin, *Intercourse*, pp. 171, 194; Dworkin, *Life and Death*, pp. 22–23, 79–80, 86, 123, 143, 173, 188–189.

[116] Dworkin, *Letters from a War Zone*, p. 139.

[117] Dworkin, *Heartbreak*, pp. 43–47.

[118] Havana Marking (April 15, 2005). "The real legacy of Andrea Dworkin" (http://www.guardian.co.uk/world/2005/apr/15/gender. politicsphilosophyandsociety). *The Guardian* (London). . Retrieved July 12, 2009.

[119] See, for example, *Letters from a War Zone*, p. 110: "One of the slurs constantly used against me by women writing in behalf of pornography under the flag of feminism in misogynist media is that I endorse a primitive biological determinism. *Woman Hating* (1974) clearly repudiates any biological determinism; so does *Our Blood* (1976), especially "The Root Cause." So does this piece, published twice, in 1978 in *Heresies* and in 1979 in *Broadsheet*. The event described in this piece ["Biological Superiority: The World's Most Dangerous and Deadly Idea"], which occurred in 1977, was fairly notorious, and so my position on biological determinism—I am against it—is generally known in the Women's Movement."

[120] See, for example, the 1995 Preface to *Intercourse*, pp. vii-x, and *Intercourse*, Chapter 7.

[121] Richards, Deborah, *Andrea Dworkin September 26, 1946 – April 9, 2005*, Apr. 12, 2005, in *H-Women*, on *Humanities and Social Sciences Net Online* (discussion list message) ("John Stoltenberg has sent these items this morning; they were prepared by Andrea Dworkin") (http:// h-net.msu.edu/cgi-bin/logbrowse.pl?trx=vx&list=H-Women&month=0504&week=b&msg=4df/tu7bqMFY6gQsMcvpAQ&user=& pw=), as accessed Oct. 8, 2010.

[122] http://www.porn-library.com/dworkin_pornography_summary.htm

[123] http://www.nostatusquo.com/ACLU/dworkin/PornAList.html

[124] *Are You Listening, Hillary? President Rape Is Who He Is*, by Andrea Dworkin, with *Note from John Stoltenberg, May 25, 2007* (http:// andreadworkin.com/hillary/index.html), as accessed Aug. 3, 2010.

[125] http://www.andreadworkin.com/audio/TraffickingConference1989_P1_M.mp3

[126] http://andreadworkin.com/audio/attgeneralcommNYC_M.mp3

[127] http://www.andreadworkin.com/audio/ViolenceAbuseWomensCitizenshipM.mp3

[128] http://andreadworkin.com/audio/strikingback/

[129] http://www.andreadworkin.com/audio/duke01.85_M.mp3

[130] http://www.andreadworkin.com/audio/dworkin_ginsberg_m.mp3

[131] Dworkin, Andrea, *Dworkin on Dworkin*, in Bell, Diane, & Renate Klein, eds., *Radically Speaking: Feminism Reclaimed* (N. Melbourne, Vic., Australia: Spinifex, 1996 (ISBN 1 875559 38 8)), pp. 203–217 (ed. Bell then prof. religion, economic development, & social justice, Coll. of the Holy Cross, Mass., U.S., & ed. Klein then sr. lecturer & dep. dir., Australian Women's Research Centre, Deakin Univ., as reprinted from *Dworkin on Dworkin*, in *Trouble and Strife*, vol. or no. 19 (Summer, 1990), pp. 2–13 (itself from Braeman, Elizabeth, and Carol Cox, title not stated, in *Off Our Backs* (probably *off our backs*) (10th birthday issue).

[132] http://www.nytimes.com/1987/05/03/books/male-and-female-men-and-women.html

[133] http://maureenmullarkey.com/essays/porn1.html

[134] http://web.archive.org/web/20030402193857/http://www.isiswomen.org/wia/wia398/vaw00006.html

[135] http://web.archive.org/web/20050306002136/http://nyc.indymedia.org/newswire/display/140928/index.php

[136] *The American Heritage Dictionary of the English Language* (Boston, Mass.: Houghton Mifflin, 3d ed. 1992 (ISBN 0-395-44895-6)), p. xii (The Usage Panel); the panel is discussed at *id.*, p. vi (Introduction).

Further reading

- Brownmiller, Susan (1999). *In Our Time: Memoir of a Revolution* (ISBN 0-385-31486-8).
- Robinson, Jeremy Mark (2008). *Andrea Dworkin* (ISBN 978-1-86171-126-7). Crescent Moon.
- Strossen, Nadine, *Defending Pornography: Free Speech, Sex, and the Fight for Women's Rights* (ISBN 0-8147-8149-7). New York University Press, 2000. (First edition New York: Scribner, 1995).

External links

- Andrea Dworkin (http://www.telegraph.co.uk/news/obituaries/culture-obituaries/1487683/Andrea-Dworkin.html) - Daily Telegraph obituary
- Portal for Andrea Dworkin's Websites (http://www.andreadworkin.com/) maintained by Nikki Craft
- Official Andrea Dworkin Online Library (http://www.nostatusquo.com/ACLU/dworkin/OnlineLibrary.html) maintained by Nikki Craft
- Andrea Dworkin Memorial Page (http://www.andreadworkin.net/) maintained by Nikki Craft
- Andrea Dworkin Quotes (http://www.brainyquote.com/quotes/authors/a/andrea_dworkin.html)
- Encyclopaedia Britannica's 300 Women who changed the world (http://www.britannica.com/women/article-9124959) – Andrea Dworkin entry
- Andrea Dworkin Papers. (http://oasis.lib.harvard.edu/oasis/deliver/deepLink?_collection=oasis&uniqueId=sch01051) Schlesinger Library (http://www.radcliffe.edu/schlesinger_library.aspx), Radcliffe Institute, Harvard University.
- Alice Shalvi, Biography of Andrea Dworkin (http://jwa.org/encyclopedia/article/dworkin-andrea), Jewish Women Encyclopedia
- Andrea Dworkin (http://www.culturalfarming.com/Porn_Parody/dworkin.html) Media praxis video tribute.

Melissa Farley

<table>
<tr><td colspan="2" align="center">**Melissa Farley**</td></tr>
<tr><td>**Born**</td><td>1942</td></tr>
<tr><td>**Residence**</td><td>San Francisco</td></tr>
<tr><td>**Nationality**</td><td>American</td></tr>
<tr><td>**Fields**</td><td>Psychology</td></tr>
<tr><td>**Institutions**</td><td>Prostitution Research and Education 1996–
Kaiser Foundation Research Institute (Oakland, CA), 1993–2000</td></tr>
<tr><td>**Alma mater**</td><td>University of Iowa (Ph.D., Counseling Psychology, 1973)
San Francisco State University (MS, Clinical Psychology, 1966)
Mills College (BA, Psychology, 1964)</td></tr>
<tr><td>**Known for**</td><td>Research on the effects of prostitution, sexual abuse, and violence against women[1]</td></tr>
</table>

Melissa Farley (born 1942) is an American clinical psychologist and researcher[1][2][3] and feminist anti-pornography and anti-prostitution activist.[4][5] Farley is best known for her studies of the effects of prostitution, trafficking, and sexual violence.

Research

Studies of prostitutes

Since 1993, Farley has researched prostitution and trafficking in several countries. She is the author of several studies of prostitutes, which claim high rates of post-traumatic stress disorder among the women studied.[3]

In a 2003 paper summarizing prostitution research carried out in locales in nine countries (Canada, Colombia, Germany, Mexico, South Africa, Thailand, Turkey, United States, and Zambia), Farley and others interviewed 854 people (782 women and girls, 44 transgendered individuals, and 28 men) currently active in prostitution or having recently exited.[6] The prostitutes interviewed came from a variety of subsets of prostitution and other sex work – street prostitutes, legal and illegal brothel workers, and prostitutes working in strip clubs were interviewed, though the prostitute populations interviewed varied between each country. Based on interviews with and questionnaires filled out by the subjects, the authors reported high rates of violence and post-traumatic stress: 71% of respondents had been physically assaulted while in prostitution, 63% had been raped, and 68% were said to meet the criteria for post-traumatic stress disorder. They also report that 89% of the respondents wished to leave prostitution, but lacked the means to do so.[6]

Farley and the coauthors of this paper state that their findings contradict what they refer to as "myths" about prostitution: that street prostitution is worse for prostitutes than other forms of prostitution, that male prostitution is different from female prostitution, that individuals who are in prostitution have freely consented to it, that most prostitutes are in prostitution as a result of drug addiction, that there is a qualitative difference between prostitution and human trafficking, and that legalizing or decriminalizing prostitution would reduce its harm.[6]

In a 1998 paper on San Francisco street prostitutes (one of the populations also included in the above-mentioned "Prostitution in Nine Countries" study), Farley and co-author Howard Barkan report notable lifetime histories of violence in the lives of those surveyed. In childhood, 57% of the respondents report sexual abuse and 49% report other physical abuse. Later in life, while in prostitution, 68% reported being raped, 82% reported being physically assaulted, and 83% reported being threatened with a weapon. Incidence and severity of post-traumatic stress disorder were reported to positively correlate with the amount of violence the individual had been subjected to. Also, 84% of the respondents reported a history of homelessness.[7]

In September 2007, Farley published a book on prostitution and sex trafficking in the state of Nevada. In the book, Farley claims that, though Nevada has legal brothels, 90% of prostitution taking place in the state is conducted in Las Vegas and Reno, both in counties where prostitution is illegal, or otherwise outside legally designated brothels. She also claims that Las Vegas in particular is a major destination for sex traffickers. She also claims that 81% of the 45 legal brothel workers she interviewed would like to leave prostitution, but in many cases are physically prevented from doing so. Farley additionally states that she had been threatened at gunpoint by one of the brothel owners during the course of the interviews.[8][9]

Her prostitution studies have been criticized by sociologist Ronald Weitzer, for alleged problems with their methodology. In particular, Weitzer was critical of what he viewed as the lack of transparency in how the interviews were conducted and how the responses were translated into statistical data, as well as the sampling bias toward highly marginalized groups of prostitutes (such as street prostitutes) and for the way the findings of Farley's studies have been more generally applied to demonstrate the harm of sex work of all kinds.[10] A 2002 study by Chudakov, et al[11] used Farley's PTSD instrument to measure the rate of post-traumatic stress disorder among sex workers in Israel. Of the fifty five consenting women interviewed, 17% met the criteria for PTSD, compared to Farley's 68% figure. Farley's critics also claim that her findings are heavily influenced by her radical feminist ideology.[12][13][14]

Farley has also been criticized for accepting significant funding from anti-prostitution organizations. She has acknowledged that 30% of funding for a prominent research project into prostitution was provided by the United States Department of State Office to Monitor and Combat Trafficking in Persons, an agency with an outspoken policy which conflates prostitution with trafficking. However, Farley has stated that such funding has not in any way swayed her research, in particular its methods or conclusions.[15]

Studies of men who buy sex

Farley is also co-author of a series of studies of men who buy sex. The first of these studies were released in April and May 2008, based on interviews with johns in Edinburgh and Chicago, respectively. Each of these reports were taken from structured interviews with over 100 men in each city, who responded to newspaper ads placed by the researchers. The study claims high rates of abusive, predatory, and dehumanizing attitudes towards prostitutes and women in general on the part of johns. The studies state that many of the men described their behavior as an addiction. The studies also stated that a large percentage of the men said that the possibility of public exposure or being placed on a sex offender registry would be effective in stopping them from buying sex from prostitutes. Similar surveys of johns in India and Cambodia are said to be forthcoming.[16][17][18]

In response to the Scottish study, a paper authored by some 15 academics and sexual health experts was submitted to the Scottish Parliament, strongly rebuking the methods and conclusions of the study. Amongst other things, the report states - "This research violates fundamental principles of human research ethics in that there is no evidence of any benefit to the population studied. Rather the purpose of the research appears to have been to vilify the population of men who were chosen to be interviewed. " In addition they criticize the work as biased, ill informed and unhelpful.[14]

Other research

Farley has also been author or co-author of several studies sponsored by Kaiser Foundation Research Institute on the long-term health effects of sexual abuse and trauma. Several of these papers report higher rates of dissociation and somatization in patients with a history of childhood sexual abuse than those without such history.[19][20][21] The frequency of such symptoms was reported to be higher in those with greater numbers of perpetrators in an individuals sexual abuse history.[20] One study reported higher rates of PTSD, emergency room and medical visits, and prescriptions in patients with a history of sexual abuse than those without. The study also reported relatively high rates of such outcomes in those with unclear memories of abuse.[21]

Activism and views

Farley is a leading proponent of the abolitionist view of prostitution[22] holding that prostitution is inherently exploitive and traumatizing, and should therefore be abolished. She is an opponent of across-the-board decriminalization of prostitution, instead advocating the "Swedish model" of prostitution laws, in which paying for sex, pimping and human trafficking are illegal, while the selling of sex is decriminalized, along with the funding of social services to "motivate prostitutes to seek help to leave their way of life." Such an approach is based on the point of view that prostitutes are the weaker partner in the transaction and are exploited.[23] She is also largely opposed to sex workers' rights activists and groups, such as COYOTE, which advocate legalizing or decriminalizing both prostitution and the purchase of sexual services.[24][25] Many of these activists are likewise strongly opposed to Farley's perspective, holding that Farley's research discredits and misrepresents women working in the sex industry and lacks accountability toward them.[25][26]

Farley is also an anti-pornography activist.[4] In 1985, she led a National Rampage Against Penthouse alongside Nikki Craft. The "Rampage" was a campaign of public destruction of bookstore-owned copies of *Penthouse* and *Hustler* (which they denounced as violent pornography). Farley was arrested 13 different times in 9 different states for these actions.[27][28][29] In March 2007, she testified in hearings about Kink.com's purchase of the San Francisco Armory, comparing the images produced by Kink.com to images of prisoner abuse at Abu Ghraib.[30][31] Farley is opposed to sadomasochism more generally, and in her essay "Ten Lies about Sadomasochism", outlines her opposition to BDSM practices, arguing that such practices are abusive, harmful, and anti-feminist.[32]

As of 2009, she is currently director of Prostitution Research and Education, a San Francisco nonprofit organization.

On April 29, 2009, Farley argued on the radio show *Intelligence Squared U.S.* for the proposition "It Is Wrong To Pay For Sex".[33]

In September 2011, Dr Calum Bennachie filed a complaint against Farley with the American Psychology Association, asking that her membership be revoked due to what he alleged were her numerous violations of ethical research standards and misrepresentation of data.[34]

Major works

- Macleod J, Farley M, Anderson L, Golding J. (2008). *Challenging men's demand for prostitution in Scotland* [35]. Glasgow: Women's Support Project. ISBN 978-0-9558976-0-3
- Farley M. (2007). *Prostitution and trafficking in Nevada: making the connections.* San Francisco: Prostitution Research and Education. ISBN 0615162053
- Farley M (ed). (2004). *Prostitution, trafficking and traumatic stress.* Binghamton, NY: Haworth Maltreatment & Trauma Press. ISBN 0789023784 (hardcover) ISBN 0789023792 (paperback)
- Farley M. (2004). "Bad for the body, bad for the heart": Prostitution harms women even if legalized or decriminalized. [36] *Violence Against Women* 10(10): 1087–1125. doi:10.1177/1077801204268607
- Farley M, Cotton A, Lynne J, Zumbeck S, Spiwak F, Reyes ME, Alvarez D, Sezgin U. (2003). Prostitution and trafficking in nine countries: Update on violence and posttraumatic stress disorder. [37] *Journal of Trauma Practice* 2(3/4):33–74. doi:10.1300/J189v02n03_03
- Farley M, Patsalides BM. (2001). Physical symptoms, posttraumatic stress disorder, and healthcare utilization of women with and without childhood physical and sexual abuse. *Psychological Reports* 89(3):595–606. doi:10.2466/PR0.89.7.595-606
- Farley M, Barkan H. (1998). Prostitution, violence, and post-traumatic stress disorder. [38] *Women & Health* 27(3):37–49. doi:10.1300/J013v27n03_03
- Farley M, Baral I, Kiremire M, Sezgin U. (1998). Prostitution in five countries: Violence and posttraumatic stress disorder. [39] *Feminism & Psychology* 8(4):405–426. doi:10.1300/J013v27n03_03
- Farley M, Keaney JC. (1997). Physical symptoms, somatization, and dissociation in women survivors of childhood sexual assault. *Women & Health* 25(3):33–45. doi:10.1300/J013v25n03_03

References

[1] "Melissa Farley: Curriculum Vitae" (http://disability-abuse.com/txt/OnlineFacultyCVs/FarleyCV.txt), 2004.
[2] "Slick S.F. posters advocate decriminalizing prostitution" (http://www.sfgate.com/cgi-bin/article.cgi?f=/e/a/1995/08/14/NEWS5272. dtl) by Kevin Foley, *San Francisco Examiner*, August 14, 1995. "Melissa Farley, a San Francisco clinical and research psychologist who helped to interview 130 local prostitutes for a survey,..."
[3] "Many Prostitutes Suffer Combat Disorder, Study Finds" (http://query.nytimes.com/gst/fullpage. html?res=9E02E6DC163DF93BA2575BC0A96E958260) by Abigail Zuger, *New York Times*, August 18, 1998. "Dr. Melissa Farley, a psychologist and researcher at the Kaiser-Permanente Medical Center in San Francisco who directed the study with colleagues from Turkey and Africa."
[4] "Prostitution: The oldest use and abuse of women" (http://findarticles.com/p/articles/mi_qa3693/is_199405/ai_n8714216/pg_3) by Melissa Farley, *off our backs*, May 1994. (*FindArticles.com* archive, p 3.) "Melissa Farley is a fiminist [sp] psychologist and antipornography activist who understands that pornography is 'pictures of prostitution'".
[5] "Sober forum, street theater on prostitution ballot issue" (http://www.sfgate.com/cgi-bin/article.cgi?f=/c/a/2004/08/31/ BAGCS8H7FV1.DTL) by Patrick Hoge, *San Francisco Chronicle*, August 31, 2004. "Melissa Farley, a San Francisco psychologist and anti-prostitution activist."
[6] Prostitution and trafficking in nine countries: Update on violence and posttraumatic stress disorder (http://www.prostitutionresearch.com/ pdf/Prostitutionin9Countries.pdf) by Melissa Farley, Ann Cotton, Jacqueline Lynne, and others, *Journal of Trauma Practice* 2(3/4):33–74, 2003. doi:10.1300/J189v02n03_03
[7] Prostitution, violence, and post-traumatic stress disorder (http://www.prostitutionresearch.com/prostitution_research/000021.html) by Melissa Farley and Howard Barkan, *Women & Health* 27(3):37–49, 1998. doi:10.1300/J013v27n03_03
[8] "Outlaw industry, ex-prostitutes say" (http://www.lvrj.com/news/9612332.html) by Lynnette Curtis, *Las Vegas Review-Journal*, September 6, 2007.
[9] "Panel: Brothels aid sex trafficking" (http://www.pahrumpvalleytimes.com/2007/Sep-07-Fri-2007/news/16519321.html) by Mark Waite, *Pahrump Valley Times*, September 7, 2007.
[10] "Flawed Theory and Method in Studies of Prostitution" (http://web.archive.org/web/20060111065947/http://www. woodhullfoundation.org/content/otherpublications/WeitzerVAW-1.pdf) by Ronald Weitzer, *Violence Against Women* 11(7): 934–949, July 2005.
[11] The motivation and mental health of sex workers. (http://cmsprod.bgu.ac.il/NR/rdonlyres/ 606501A6-2077-4281-BB7D-1B554A565223/90420/motivationofsexworkersEnglishChudakovCwikel.pdf) by Chudakov B, Ilan K, Belmaker RH, Cwikel J. *Journal of Sex and Marital Therapy* 28(4):305–15, 2002. doi:10.1080/00926230290001439.
[12] Weitzer, "Flawed Theory and Method in Studies of Prostitution" (above-cited); "The articles in question are by Jody Raphael and Deborah Shapiro (2004), Melissa Farley (2004), and Janice Raymond (2004). At least two of the authors (Farley and Raymond) are activists involved in the antiprostitution campaign. [...] The three articles are only the most recent examples in a long line of writings on the sex industry by authors who adopt an extreme version of radical feminist theory—extreme in the sense that it is absolutist, doctrinaire, and unscientific."
[13] Letter to Ambassador John Miller (http://www.genderhealth.org/pubs/LtrMillerTrafficking.pdf) by Ann Jordan and others, *Center for Health and Gender Equity*, April 21, 2005, p 4.
[14] "A Commentary on 'Challenging Men's Demand for Prostitution in Scotland': A Research Report Based on Interviews with 110 Men who Bought Women in Prostitution, (Jan Macleod, Melissa Farley, Lynn Anderson, Jacqueline Golding, 2008)" (http://myweb.dal.ca/ mgoodyea/Documents/Client studies/FarleyCritique-2.doc) by Teela Sanders, Jane Scoular, Michael Goodyear, and others, April 29, 2008. "The researchers were defined as people wanting to end violence against women - but presumably this may introduce bias into how the research was run. If you are asking someone to disclose buying sex but you openly disagree with this how can you hear what they say?"

[15] Response to Melissa Farley (http://swopeast.blogspot.com/2007/09/response-to-melissa-farley.html) by Jill Brenneman, *SWOP East* (website), September 18, 2007

[16] "Sex industry in Scotland: Inside the deluded minds of the punters" (http://www.dailyrecord.co.uk/news/scottish-news/2008/04/28/sex-industry-in-scotland-inside-the-deluded-minds-of-the-punters-86908-20397545/) by Annie Brown, *Daily Record*, April 28, 2008. Accessed 2008-05-11.

[17] *Challenging men's demand for prostitution in Scotland* (http://whiteribbonscotland.files.wordpress.com/2008/04/challenging_mens_demand.pdf) by J Macleod, M Farley, L Anderson, and J Golding, *Women's Support Project*, April 2008. ISBN 978-0-9558976-0-3.

[18] "Some men say using prostitutes is an addiction" (http://www.chicagotribune.com/news/local/chi-sex-trade-studymay06,0,3574868.story) by David Heinzmann, *Chicago Tribune*, May 5, 2008. Accessed 2008-05-11.

[19] Keaney JC, Farley M. (1996). Dissociation in an outpatient sample of women reporting childhood sexual abuse. *Psychological Reports* 78(1): 59–65. doi:10.2466/PR0.78.1.59-65. PMID 8839296.

[20] Farley M, Keaney JC. (1997). Physical symptoms, somatization, and dissociation in women survivors of childhood sexual assault. *Women & Health* 25(3): 33–45. doi:10.1300/J013v25n03 03.

[21] Farley M, Patsalides BM. (2001). Physical symptoms, posttraumatic stress disorder, and healthcare utilization of women with and without childhood physical and sexual abuse. Psychological Reports 89(3): 595–606. doi:10.2466/PR0.89.7.595-606. PMID 9273982.

[22] "Feminists fight over prostitution" (http://toledoblade.com/apps/pbcs.dll/article?AID=/20060924/COLUMNIST03/609240366/) by Roberta deBoer, *Toledo Blade*, September 24, 2006.

[23] "Prostitution, trafficking, and cultural amnesia: What we must not know in order to keep the business of sexual exploitation running smoothly" (http://www.prostitutionresearch.com/pdfs/FarleyYaleLaw2006.pdf) by Melissa Farley, *Yale Journal of Law and Feminism* 18(1):109–144, Spring 2006.

[24] "Ex-prostitutes' quilt honors slain women" by Associated Press, *Las Vegas Review-Journal*, April 13, 1994, p 14.

[25] "Prostitution: Pro or Con?" (http://www.portlandmercury.com/portland/Content?oid=26820) by Katia Dunn, *Portland Mercury*, May 9, 2002.

[26] "A victimless crime?" (http://archive.unlvrebelyell.com/article.php?ID=11040) by Alicia Portillo, *The Rebel Yell* (UNLV student newspaper), September 20, 2007.

[27] "Fighting Femicide in the United States: The Rampage Against Penthouse" (http://www.nostatusquo.com/ACLU/Porn/rampage1femicide1991.pdf) by Melissa Farley, in Jill Radford and Diana E. H. Russell (eds.), *Femicide: The Politics of Woman Killing*, New York: Twayne Publishers, 1992.

[28] "2 Groups on 'Midwestern Rampage' 'Violent Pornography' Protested" by Terry Hyland, *Omaha World-Herald*, February 25, 1985.

[29] "Protesters of Porn Guilty of Destruction", *Omaha World-Herald*, March 10, 1985.

[30] "San Francisco Planning Commission - Special Public Hearing" (http://sanfrancisco.granicus.com/MediaPlayer.php?view_id=20&clip_id=3256), *SFGTV*, March 8, 2007. (link to streaming Windows Media video and downloadable MP3 audio)

[31] "Kink.Com in San Francisco: Women and Gay Men's Abu Ghraib" (http://www.prostitutionresearch.com/blog/2007/02/kinkcom_in_san_francisco_women.html) by Melissa Farley, *Traffick Jamming* (blog), February 8, 2007.

[32] "Ten Lies About Sadomasochism" (http://www.mediawatch.com/wordpress/?p=21) by Melissa Farley, *Sinister Wisdom* #50, Summer/Fall 1993, p 29-37. (Archived at *MediaWatch.com*.)

[33] Is It Wrong To Pay For Sex? (http://www.npr.org/templates/story/story.php?storyId=103639465) 2009-04-29

[34] http://cybersolidaires.typepad.com/files/complaint-to-apa-against-mfarley.pdf

[35] http://whiteribbonscotland.files.wordpress.com/2008/04/challenging_mens_demand.pdf

[36] http://www.prostitutionresearch.com/FarleyVAW.pdf

[37] http://www.prostitutionresearch.com/pdf/Prostitutionin9Countries.pdf

[38] http://www.prostitutionresearch.com/prostitution_research/000021.html

[39] http://www.prostitutionresearch.com/prostitution_research/000020.html

External links

By Melissa Farley

- Prostitution Research and Education (http://www.prostitutionresearch.com/)
  - Prostitution Research (http://www.prostitutionresearch.com/c-prostitution-research.html) – select publications.
  - Traffick Jamming (http://www.prostitutionresearch.com/blog/) – Melissa Farley's blog.
- Melissa Farley CV (http://www.prostitutionresearch.com/MFarley CV.pdf), 2008. – Includes list of publications as of 2008.
- "The Demand for Prostitution" (http://www.captivedaughters.org/demanddynamics/demandforprostitution.htm) by Melissa Farley, *Captive Daughters* (website).
- Letter to the Editor (http://www.nostatusquo.com/ACLU/ohBROTHER/farley.html) by Melissa Farley , *Changing Men*, September 29 and November 6, 1992.
- "Prostitution: The oldest use and abuse of women" (http://findarticles.com/p/articles/mi_qa3693/is_199405/ai_n8714216/pg_1) by Melissa Farley, *off our backs*, May 1994. (Archived at *FindArticles.com*.)
- "Why I Made the Choice To Become A Prostitute" (http://www.nostatusquo.com/ACLU/Porn/WhyIMade.html) by Nikki Craft and Melissa Farley, *Always Causing Legal Unrest* (website), 1996.
- "Attitudes Toward Prostitution and Acceptance of Rape Myths" (http://www.caase.org/uploads/File/Cotton=Farley=Baron.pdf) by Ann Cotton, Melissa Farley, and Robert Baron, *Journal of Applied Social Psychology* 32:1–8, 2002.
- "Prostitution of Indigenous Women: Sex Inequality and the Colonization of Canada's First Nations Women" (http://www.cwis.org/fwj/61/prostitution_of_indigenous_women.htm) by Melissa Farley and Jacqueline Lynne, *Fourth World Journal* 6(1):1–29, 2005.

- "Prostitution and sex trafficking as severe forms of violence against women" (http://web.archive.org/web/20060504185243/http://sisyphe.org/breve.php3?id_breve=440) by Melissa Farely, *Sisyphe* (website), September 9, 2005. (Archived at Wayback Machine, May 4, 2006.)
- "Renting an Organ for Ten Minutes: What Tricks Tell Us about Prostitution, Pornography, and Trafficking" (http://www.caase.org/uploads/File/FarleyRentinganOrgan11-06.pdf) by Melissa Farley, from: *Pornography: Driving the Demand in International Sex Trafficking*, Captive Daughters Media, 2007. ISBN 1425758851
- The Myth of the Victimless Crime (http://www.nytimes.com/2008/03/12/opinion/12farley.html?ref=opinion) by Melissa Farley and Victor Malarek, *New York Times*, March 12, 2008.

Criticism of Melissa Farley

- "A Feminist View That All Sexworkers are Abused and Sick" (http://www.sexwork.com/whatisnew/farley.html), *Sexwork.org*, 2002.
- "The pimps are coming!: Opponents of Berkeley's prostitution measure use alarmist rhetoric" (http://www.sfbg.com/39/04/news_prostitution.html) by Ann Harrison, *San Francisco Bay Guardian*, October 27, 2004.
- "Nevada Views: Vegas and the sex industry" (http://www.lvrj.com/opinion/9812702.html) by Kate Hausbeck, Barbara Brents, and Crystal Jackson, *Las Vegas Review-Journal*, September 16, 2007.
- Review of *Prostitution and Trafficking in Nevada, Making the Connections* (http://deepthroated.wordpress.com/2007/09/17/review-of-prostitution-and-trafficking-in-nevada-making-the-connections/) by Barbara Brents, *Bound, Not Gagged* (blog), September 17, 2007.
- "Bewildered, academics pore over sex-trade hysteria" (http://www.lasvegassun.com/news/2008/jan/31/bewildered-academics-pore-over-sex-trade-hysteria/) by Abigail Goldman, *Las Vegas Sun*, January 31, 2008.

Debates between Melissa Farley and others

- "'Bad for the Body, Bad for the Heart': Prostitution Harms Women Even If Legalized or Decriminalized" (http://www.prostitutionresearch.com/FarleyVAW.pdf) by Melissa Farley, *Violence Against Women* 10(10): 1087-1125, October 2004.
  - "Flawed Theory and Method in Studies of Prostitution" (http://web.archive.org/web/20060111065947/http://www.woodhullfoundation.org/content/otherpublications/WeitzerVAW-1.pdf) by Ronald Weitzer, *Violence Against Women* 11(7): 934–949, July 2005.
  - "Prostitution Harms Women Even if Indoors: Reply to Weitzer" (http://www.nostatusquo.com/farley/FarleyResponse.pdf) by Melissa Farley, *Violence Against Women* 11(7): 950–964, July 2005.
  - "Rehashing Tired Claims About Prostitution: A Response to Farley and Raphael and Shapiro" (http://www.webcitation.org/query?url=http://www.geocities.com/wikispace/weitzer.2005b.pdf&date=2009-10-26+03:11:46) by Ronald Weitzer, *Violence Against Women* 11(7): 971–977, July 2005.
- "Oversexed" (http://www.thenation.com/doc/20050829/nathan) by Debbie Nathan, *The Nation*, August 11, 2005.
  - "Unequal" (http://action.web.ca/home/catw/readingroom.shtml?x=81265) by Melissa Farley, *Coalition Against Trafficking in Women* (website), August 30, 2005.
- "It's Wrong to Pay For Sex" (http://www.npr.org/templates/story/story.php?storyId=103639465), Intelligence Squared, April 21, 2009.

Panel and symposium discussions

- "Sex For Sale Symposium: Panel on Prostitution" (http://ylsqtss.law.yale.edu/qtmedia/events06/sexforsalepanel1.mov), Yale Law School, February 4, 2006. (Quicktime MOV video. Archived at *Yale Journal of Law and Feminism* website.)

News articles, reports, and editorials

- "Many Prostitutes Suffer Combat Disorder, Study Finds" (http://query.nytimes.com/gst/fullpage.html?res=9E02E6DC163DF93BA2575BC0A96E958260) by Abigail Zuger, *New York Times*, August 18, 1998.
- "Former Prostitutes Wage War Against Prostitution" (http://www.klas-tv.com/Global/story.asp?S=7029088) by Edward Lawrence, *KLAS-TV Eyewitness News*, September 5, 2007.
- "City as Predator" (http://select.nytimes.com/2007/09/04/opinion/04herbert.html) by Bob Herbert, *New York Times*, September 4, 2007.
- "Escape From Las Vegas" (http://select.nytimes.com/2007/09/08/opinion/08herbert.html) by Bob Herbert, *New York Times*, September 8, 2007.

- "Fantasies, Well-Meant" (http://select.nytimes.com/2007/09/11/opinion/11herbert.html) by Bob Herbert, *New York Times*, September 11, 2007.
- "'It's like you sign a contract to be raped'" (http://www.guardian.co.uk/g2/story/0,,2164107,00.html) by Julie Bindel, *The Guardian*, September 7, 2007.

Sheila Jeffreys

Sheila Jeffreys (born 1948) is a lesbian feminist scholar and political activist, known for her analysis of the history and politics of sexuality in Britain. She is a professor in Political Science at the University of Melbourne in Australia. Jeffreys's argument that the "sexual revolution" on men's terms contributed less to women's freedom than to their continued oppression has both commanded respect and attracted intense criticism.[1][2][3][4] Jeffreys argues that transsexuals reproduce oppressive gender roles and mutilate their bodies through sex reassignment surgery. Some of Jeffrey's other controversial positions are that lesbian culture has been negatively impacted by emulating the sexist influence of the gay male subculture of dominant/submissive sexuality, and that women suffering pain in pursuit of beauty is a form of submission to patriarchal sadism.

In 1979, Jeffreys helped write *Love Your Enemy? The Debate Between Heterosexual Feminism and Political Lesbianism*, a pamphlet that offered a definition of a political lesbian: "We do think... that all feminists can and should be lesbians. Our definition of a political lesbian is a woman-identified woman who does not fuck men. It does not mean compulsory sexual activity with women."[5] Jeffreys was one of several contributors to *The sexual dynamics of history: men's power, women's resistance*, an anthology of feminist writings about gender relations published in 1983 under the name "London Feminist History Group." Jeffreys wrote the last of this book's eleven chapters, *Sex reform and anti-feminism in the 1920s.*[6]

Jeffreys's best known historical work is *The Spinster and Her Enemies: Feminism and Sexuality 1880-1930*, published in 1985. It challenges the view that the sexual puritanism of Victorian England was displaced by the scientifically enlightened ideas of sexologists such as Sigmund Freud and Havelock Ellis. It examines late 19th century and early 20th century feminist campaigns against child abuse and prostitution, identifying the New Woman vision espoused by spokesmen for sexology as a male backlash strategy. Jeffreys argues that these concepts were authoritarian and interpreted women's sexuality to conform to men's preferences. She traces later adaptations of these concepts made to fit changing social conditions: the New Woman was modified to accommodate wartime pro-natalist imperatives, and the sexually hedonistic Flapper Girl was invented to move women out of traditional male roles assumed by default during the World War I period, which had allowed them greater independence in paid work at home and at the front.

In *Anticlimax: A Feminist Perspective on the Sexual Revolution*, published in 1990, Jeffreys criticises popular prescriptions for women's sexuality from the 1950s on in key texts including pornography, sex manuals and surveys, and best-selling novels. Having spent most of her life in the United Kingdom, Jeffreys moved to Australia in the early 1990s.

The Lesbian Heresy was published in 1993.[7] In it Jeffreys is highly critical of sadomasochistic practices that involved women. One author involved in sadomasochism cites Jeffreys' views in this book as an example of the "simplistic and dualistic thinking" among anti-sadomasochism campaigners, when she describes sadomasochism as "male supremacist", a reenactment of heterosexual male dominance and women's oppression, which glorifies violence and uses women's bodies as a sex aid, and as anti-lesbian and fascistic. The author points out that Jeffreys ignores that some heterosexual women may enjoy sex, and that 'tops' may be women who work hard to give their 'bottoms' pleasure, rather than the passive recipients of sex in the way she describes.[8]

Jeffreys book *The Political Economy of the Global Sex Trade: The Industrial Vagina*, was published in February 2009.[9][10] It describes the globalisation of the sex industry, and includes a controversial description of marriage as a form of prostitution; in her article on Jeffreys, Julie Bindel quotes her: "the right of men to women's bodies for sexual use has not gone but remains an assumption at the basis of heterosexual relationships", and explains that she draws out more obvious links between marriage and prostitution, such as mail-order brides, which she sees as a form of trafficking.[11]

Jeffreys has received attention for her views on transgender, transsexualism and gender reassignment. In interview, Bindel explains that Jeffreys argues that transsexual surgery "is an extension of the beauty industry offering cosmetic solutions to deeper rooted problems", that in a society without gender this would be unnecessary. She describes 'transgender' surgeries as 'mutilation', and forced feminization pornography as portraying a view of women as less powerful.[5]

Bibliography

- Jeffreys, Sheila. *Anticlimax : a feminist perspective on the sexual revolution.* Washington Square, N.Y. : New York University Press, 1991. ISBN 0-8147-4179-7 (cloth). ISBN 0-8147-4180-0 (pbk.).
- Jeffreys, Sheila. *The lesbian heresy : a feminist perspective on the lesbian sexual revolution.* North Melbourne : Spinifex, 1993. ISBN 1-875559-17-5
- Jeffreys, Sheila. *The spinster and her enemies : feminism and sexuality, 1880-1930.* [New ed.] North Melbourne : Spinifex Press, 1997. ISBN 1-875559-63-9
- Jeffreys, Sheila. *Unpacking queer politics : a lesbian feminist perspective.* Cambridge : Polity ; Oxford : Blackwell, 2003. ISBN 0-7456-2837-0 (hbk.), ISBN 0-7456-2838-9 (pbk.).
- Jeffreys, Sheila. *Beauty and Misogyny : Harmful Cultural Practices in the West.* London : Routledge, 2005. ISBN 0-415-35183-9 (hbk.). ISBN 0-415-35182-0 (pbk.).
- Jeffreys, Sheila. *The Industrial Vagina : The political economy of the sex trade.* London : Routledge, 2009. ISBN 0-415-41232-3 (hbk.). ISBN 0-415-41233-1 (pbk.).

References

[1] SAMOIS (1987). *Coming to Power: Writings and Graphics on Lesbian S/M.* Boston: Alyson Publications. p. 88. ISBN 0-932870-28-7.
[2] Vance, Carole S. (1992). *Pleasure and Danger: Exploring Female Sexuality.* London: Pandora. p. 302. ISBN 0 04 440867 6.
[3] Gilbert, Harriett. (1993). *The Sexual Imagination from Acker to Zola: A Feminist Companion.* London: Jonathan Cape. p. 133. ISBN 0-224-03535-5.
[4] Denfeld, Rene. (1995). *The New Victorians: A Young Woman's Challenge to the Old Feminist Order.* New York: Warner Books. p. 35. ISBN 1-86373-789-8.
[5] Bindel, Julie (2 July 2005). "The ugly side of beauty" (http://www.guardian.co.uk/world/2005/jul/02/gender. politicsphilosophyandsociety). *Guardian.* .
[6] London Feminist History Group (1983). *The Sexual Dynamics of History: Men's power, women's resistance.* London: Pluto Press. p. vi. ISBN 0-86104-711-7.
[7] Jeffreys, Sheila (1993). *The Lesbian Heresy: A Feminist Perspective on the Lesbian Sexual Revolution.* Spinifex Press.
[8] Stein, Atara (1998-09-28). "'Without Contraries Is No Progression': S/M, Bi-nary Thinking, and the Lesbian Purity Test" (http://books. google.com/?id=seZp6LNoF60C&pg=PA53&lpg=PA53&dq=sheila+jeffreys+BDSM). In Atkins, Dawn. *Lesbian Sex Scandals.* Haworth Press. 1998. p. 53. ISBN 9780789005489. .
[9] The Political Economy of the Global Sex Trade (http://www.amazon.com/dp/0415412331)
[10] http://www.abc.net.au/rn/breakfast/stories/2009/2498297.htm ABC Radion National Interview with Jefferys regarding her new book
[11] Bindel, Julie (12 Nov 2008). "'Marriage is a form of prostitution'" (http://www.guardian.co.uk/lifeandstyle/2008/nov/12/ women-prostitution-marriage-sex-trade). *Guardian.* .

External links

- "Allowing Alex's sex change shows up a gender-biased Family Court" - Article by Jeffreys (http://www. onlineopinion.com.au/view.asp?article=2162)
- "Body modification as self-mutilation by proxy" - Article by Jeffreys (http://www.onlineopinion.com.au/ view.asp?article=4312)
- "How Orgasm Politics has hijacked the women's movement" - Essay by Jeffreys (http://www. ontheissuesmagazine.com/s96orgasm.html)
- "Trafficking in Women vs. Prostitution: A False Distinction" - Keynote address at Townsville International Women's Conference (http://www.nswp.org/pdf/JEFFREYS-WINTER.PDF)
- Critical review of Jeffreys's book Anticlimax (http://www.greenleft.org.au/back/1991/34/34p19.htm)
- Critical review of Jeffeys's book The Lesbian Heresy (http://glamourousrags.dymphna.net/reviewjeffreys. html)
- Critical review of Jeffrey's book The Idea of Prostitution (http://www.scarletalliance.org.au/Reviews/ hanson98/)
- Interview with The Guardian (http://books.guardian.co.uk/departments/politicsphilosophyandsociety/story/ 0,,1519268,00.html)
- Jeffreys's official Melbourne University home page (http://www.ssps.unimelb.edu.au/about/staff/profiles/ jeffreys)

Catharine MacKinnon

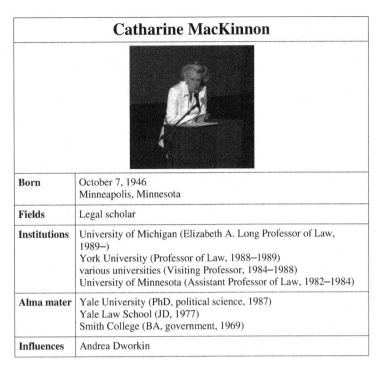

Catharine MacKinnon	
Born	October 7, 1946 Minneapolis, Minnesota
Fields	Legal scholar
Institutions	University of Michigan (Elizabeth A. Long Professor of Law, 1989–) York University (Professor of Law, 1988–1989) various universities (Visiting Professor, 1984–1988) University of Minnesota (Assistant Professor of Law, 1982–1984)
Alma mater	Yale University (PhD, political science, 1987) Yale Law School (JD, 1977) Smith College (BA, government, 1969)
Influences	Andrea Dworkin

Catharine Alice MacKinnon (born October 7, 1946) is an American feminist, scholar, lawyer, teacher and activist.

Biography

MacKinnon was born in Minnesota. Her mother is Elizabeth Valentine Davis; her father, George E. MacKinnon was a lawyer, congressman (1946 to 1949), and judge on the U.S. Court of Appeals for the D.C. Circuit (1969 to 1995). She also has two younger brothers.

MacKinnon became the third generation of her family to attend her mother's alma mater, Smith College. She graduated at the top 2% of her class at Smith and moved on to receive her J.D. and Ph.D. from Yale University. She was the recipient of a National Science Foundation fellowship while at Yale Law School.

MacKinnon was engaged to Jeffrey Moussaieff Masson for several years during the early 1990s, though the relationship subsequently ended. She has refused to discuss the relationship in later interviews.[1][2]

MacKinnon is the Elizabeth A. Long Professor of Law at the University of Michigan Law School.[3] In 2007, she served as the Roscoe Pound Visiting Professor of Law at Harvard Law School.[4]

MacKinnon is a highly cited legal scholar.[5][6] She has frequently been a visiting professor at other universities and regularly appears in public speaking events. On February 10, 2005, MacKinnon attended the premiere of *Inside Deep Throat* (in which she is interviewed) and took part in a panel discussion after the film in order to criticize it.[7][8] On April 29, 2009, MacKinnon argued on the radio show *Intelligence Squared U.S.* for the proposition "it's wrong to pay for sex."[9]

Ideas and activism

MacKinnon's ideas may be divided into three central—though overlapping and ongoing—areas of focus: (1) sexual harassment, (2) pornography, and (3) international work. She has also devoted attention to social and political theory and methodology.[10]

Sexual harassment

According to an article published by Deborah Dinner in the March/April 2006 issue of *Legal Affairs*, MacKinnon first became interested in issues concerning sexual harassment when she heard that an administrative assistant at Cornell University resigned after being refused a transfer when she complained of her supervisor's harassing behavior, and then was denied unemployment benefits because she quit for 'personal' reasons. It was at a consciousness-raising session about this and other women's workplace experiences that the term sexual harassment was first coined.[11]

In 1977, MacKinnon graduated from Yale Law School after having written a paper on the topic of sexual harassment for Professor Thomas I. Emerson. Two years later, MacKinnon published "Sexual Harassment of Working Women," arguing that sexual harassment is a form of sex discrimination under Title VII of the Civil Rights Act of 1964 and any other sex discrimination prohibition. While working on "Sexual Harassment", MacKinnon shared draft copies with attorneys litigating early sexual harassment cases, including Nadine Traub, who represented Yale undergraduates in Alexander v. Yale, the first test case of MacKinnon's legal theory.[12][13]

In her book, MacKinnon argued that sexual harassment is sex discrimination because the act reinforces the social inequality of women to men (see, for example, pp. 116–18, 174). She distinguishes between two types of sexual harassment (see pp. 32–42): 1) "quid pro quo," meaning sexual harassment "in which sexual compliance is exchanged, or proposed to be exchanged, for an employment opportunity (p. 32)" and 2) the type of harassment that "arises when sexual harassment is a persistent condition of work (p. 32)." In 1980, the Equal Employment Opportunity Commission followed MacKinnon's framework in adopting guidelines prohibiting sexual harassment by prohibiting both quid pro quo harassment and hostile work environment harassment (see 29 C.F.R. § 1604.11(a)).

In 1986, the Supreme Court held in *Meritor Savings Bank v. Vinson* that sexual harassment may violate laws against sex discrimination. In *Meritor*, the Court also recognized the distinction between quid pro quo sexual harassment and hostile work place harassment. Wrote MacKinnon in a 2002 article: "'Without question,' then-Justice Rehnquist wrote for a unanimous Court, 'when a supervisor sexually harasses a subordinate because of the subordinate's sex, that supervisor "discriminate[s]" on the basis of sex.' The D.C. Circuit, and women, had won. A new common law rule was established."[14]

MacKinnon's book *Sexual Harassment of Working Women: A Case of Sex Discrimination* is the eighth most-cited American legal book published since 1978, according to a study published by Fred Shapiro in January 2000.

Pornography

In 1980, Linda Boreman (who had appeared in the pornographic film *Deep Throat* as "Linda Lovelace") stated that her ex-husband Chuck Traynor had violently coerced her into making Deep Throat and other pornographic films. Boreman made her charges public for the press corps at a press conference, together with MacKinnon, members of Women Against Pornography, and feminist writer Andrea Dworkin offering statements in support. After the press conference, Dworkin, MacKinnon, Gloria Steinem, and Boreman began discussing the possibility of using federal civil rights law to seek damages from Traynor and the makers of *Deep Throat*. Linda Boreman was interested, but backed off after Steinem discovered that the statute of limitations for a possible suit had passed (Brownmiller 337).

MacKinnon and Dworkin, however, continued to discuss civil rights litigation as a possible approach to combatting pornography. MacKinnon opposed traditional arguments against pornography based on the idea of morality or sexual innocence, as well as the use of traditional criminal obscenity law to suppress pornography. Instead of condemning pornography for violating "community standards" of sexual decency or modesty, they characterized pornography as a form of sex discrimination, and sought to give women the right to seek damages under civil rights law.

In 1983, the Minneapolis city government hired MacKinnon and Dworkin to draft an antipornography civil rights ordinance as an amendment to the Minneapolis city civil rights ordinance. The amendment defined pornography as a civil rights violation against women, and allowed women who claimed harm from pornography to sue the producers and distributors for damages in civil court. The law was passed twice by the Minneapolis city council but vetoed by the mayor. Another version of the ordinance passed in Indianapolis, Indiana, in 1984.

This ordinance was ruled unconstitutional by the Seventh Circuit Court of Appeals. MacKinnon continued to support the civil rights approach in her writing and activism, and supported anti-pornography feminists who organized later campaigns in Cambridge, Massachusetts (1985) and Bellingham, Washington (1988) to pass versions of the ordinance by voter initiative.

MacKinnon also wrote in the *Harvard Civil Rights-Civil Liberties Law Review* in 1985:

> And as you think about the assumption of consent that follows women into pornography, look closely some time for the skinned knees, the bruises, the welts from the whippings, the scratches, the gashes. Many of them are not simulated. One relatively soft core pornography model said, "I knew the pose was right when it hurt." It certainly seems important to the audiences that the events in the pornography be real. For this reason, pornography becomes a motive for murder, as in "snuff" films in which someone is tortured to death to make a sex film. They exist."[15]

MacKinnon represented Linda Susan Boreman (better known under her stage name of Linda Lovelace) from 1980 until her death in 2002.

Civil libertarians frequently find MacKinnon's theories objectionable (see "Criticisms" section). They have also argued that there is no evidence that sexually explicit media encourages or promotes violence against, or other measurable harm of, women,[16] but that view is not universally supported.[17]

International work

In February 1992, the Supreme Court of Canada largely accepted MacKinnon's theories of equality, hate propaganda, and pornography, citing extensively from a brief she co-authored in a ruling against Manitoba pornography distributor Donald Butler.

The *Butler* decision was controversial; it is sometimes implied that shipments of Dworkin's book *Pornography* were seized by Canadian customs agents under this ruling, as well as books by Marguerite Duras and David Leavitt;[18] the books were indeed seized by customs, but not as a consequence of *Butler*.[19] Successful *Butler* prosecutions have been undertaken against the lesbian sadomasochistic magazine *Bad Attitude*, as well as the owners of a gay and lesbian bookstore for selling it. Canadian authorities have also raided an art gallery and confiscated controversial paintings depicting child abuse. Many free speech and gay rights activists allege the law is selectively enforced, targeting the LGBT community.

MacKinnon has represented Bosnian and Croatian women against Serbs accused of genocide since 1992. She was co-counsel, representing named plaintiff S. Kadic, in the lawsuit *Kadic v. Karadzic* and won a jury verdict of $745 million in New York City on August 10, 2000. The lawsuit (under the United States' Alien Tort Statute) also established forced prostitution and forced impregnation as legally actionable acts of genocide. In MacKinnon's view, traditional approaches to human rights gloss over abuses specific to women (e.g., sexual violence), both in wartime and peacetime.

MacKinnon has also worked to change laws, or their interpretation and application in Mexico, Japan, Israel, and India. In 2001, MacKinnon was named co-director of the Lawyers Alliance for Women (LAW) Project, an initiative of Equality Now, an international non-governmental organization.

Political theory

MacKinnon's work largely focuses on the meaning of equality in law and life. Traditional equality employed the Aristotelian notion of equality—that is, the treatment of likes alike, unlikes unalike. MacKinnon believes that this fails to recognize that subordination of groups and existing hierarchy in society results in differences perceived as natural. The law, or other groups with power, then justifies distinctions based on these differences. In MacKinnon's theories, the opposite of equality is not difference but hierarchy as social constructs. "Equality thus requires promoting equality of status for historically subordinated groups, dismantling group hierarchy." In MacKinnon's view, this requires a substantive approach to equality jurisprudence in its examination of hierarchy, whereas before, abstract notions of equality sufficed.

MacKinnon writes about the interrelations between theory and practice, recognizing that women's experiences have, for the most part, been ignored in both arenas. Furthermore, she uses Marxism to critique certain points in feminist theory and uses feminism to criticize Marxist theory.[20]

MacKinnon understands epistemology as theories of knowing and politics as theories of power. She explains, "Having power means, among other things, that when someone says, 'this is how it is,' it is taken as being that way. . . . Powerlessness means that when you say 'this is how it is,' it is not taken as being that way. This makes articulating silence, perceiving the presence of absence, believing those who have been socially stripped of credibility, critically contextualizing what passes for simple fact, necessary to the epistemology of a politics of the powerless."[21]

In 1996, Fred Shapiro calculated that "Feminism, Marxism, Method, and the State: Toward Feminist Jurisprudence," 8 Signs 635 (1983), was the 96th most cited article in law reviews even though it was published in a nonlegal journal.[22]

Criticisms

During the so-called "Feminist Sex Wars" in the 1980s, feminists opposing anti-pornography stances, such as Ellen Willis and Carole Vance, began referring to themselves as "pro-sex" or "sex-positive feminists". Sex positive feminists and anti-pornography feminists have debated over the implicit and explicit meanings of these labels. Sex-positive feminists claimed that anti-pornography ordinances contrived by MacKinnon and Dworkin called for the removal, censorship, or control over sexually explicit material.[23] The "sex wars" resulted in the feminist movement being split into two opposing camps over questions about pornography, consent, sexual freedom, and the relationship of free speech to equality.

Anti-pornography ordinances authored by MacKinnon and Dworkin in the United States sought for harm against victims, in relation to pornography, to be made actionable. Soon afterwards, obscenity laws passed in Canada (1985), and books and materials that fell under the new definition of pornography were removed. The Canadian Supreme Court decision R. v. Butler (1992), which upheld these laws, drew heavily on MacKinnon's arguments that pornography is a form of sex discrimination. MacKinnon has written in support of this trend in Canadian anti-pornography law, though at the same time, holding that Canada should abandon traditional obscenity law entirely in favor of a civil rights approach. She has also distanced herself from the selective enforcement of Canadian obscenity law against gays and lesbians, holding that anti-pornography laws should make no distinction between gay and heterosexual pornography.[24][25]

Books

- *Sexual Harassment of Working Women: A Case of Sex Discrimination* (1979) ISBN 0-300-02299-9 . OCLC 3912752.
- *Feminism Unmodified: Discourses on Life and Law* (1987) ISBN 0-674-29874-8 . OCLC 157005506.
- *Pornography and Civil Rights: A New Day for Women's Equality* (1988) ISBN 0-9621849-0-X . OCLC 233530845.
- *Toward a Feminist Theory of the State* (1989) ISBN 0-674-89646-7 . OCLC 26545325.
- *Only Words* (1993) ISBN 0-674-63933-2 . OCLC 28067216.
- (co-editor) *In Harm's Way: The Pornography Civil Rights Hearings*, edited by C. A. MacKinnon and A. Dworkin (1997) ISBN 0-674-44579-1 . OCLC 37418262.
- *Women's Lives, Men's Laws* (2005) ISBN 0-674-01540-1 . OCLC 55494875.
- *Are Women Human?: And Other International Dialogues*. Cambridge: Harvard Univ. Press, 2006 . ISBN 0674021878. OCLC 62085505. (currently a nominee for the Bookseller/Diagram Prize for Oddest Title of the Year.[26])

For a more complete list, see listing [27].

Court cases

- *Meritor Savings Bank v. Vinson*, 477 U.S. 57 (1986)
- *American Booksellers Ass'n, Inc. v. Hudnut* [28] (alternate URL [29]) 771 F.2d 323 (7th Cir. 1985), aff'd, 475 U.S. 1001 (1986)
- *Andrews v. Law Society of British Columbia* [1989] 1 S.C.R. 143
- *R. v. Keegstra*, [1990] 3 S.C.R. 697 (*See also* James Keegstra)
- *R. v. Butler*, [1992] 1 S.C.R. 452
- *Kadic v Karadzic* [30] Alternate URL [31] 70 F.3rd 232 (2nd Cir. 1995), rehearing denied, 74 F.3rd 377 (2nd Cir. 1996), cert. denied, 518 U.S. 1005 (1996).

Related cases

- *R. A. V. v. City of St. Paul* MacKinnon filed an amicus brief arguing that an anti-hate speech statute should be upheld based on an equality argument.
- *Oncale v. Sundowner Offshore Services* MacKinnon filed an amicus brief in support of the plaintiff, Joseph Oncale.
- *Doe v. Karadzic* [32] (93 Civ. 878) (scroll down)

References

[1] Smith, Dinitia (1993-03-22). "Love is Strange: The Crusading Feminist and the Repentant Womanizer" (http://books.google.com/ books?id=61MAAAAAMBAJ&lpg=PA36&pg=PA36#v=onepage&q=&f=false). *New York* **26** (12): pp. 36–43. . Retrieved 2010-02-14. (cover (http://books.google.com/books?id=61MAAAAAMBAJ&lpg=PP1&pg=PP1#v=onepage&q=&f=false))

[2] "Are women human?" (http://www.guardian.co.uk/world/2006/apr/12/gender.politicsphilosophyandsociety) by Stuart Jeffries, *The Guardian*, April 12, 2006.

[3] University of Michigan faculty biography (http://cgi2.www.law.umich.edu/_FacultyBioPage/facultybiopagenew.asp?ID=219)

[4] Harvard webpage (http://www.law.harvard.edu/faculty/directory/index.html?id=734) 2007

[5] ISI Highly Cited Author - Catharine A. MacKinnon (http://hcr3.isiknowledge.com/author.cgi?id=3663)

[6] Catharine MacKinnon (http://web.archive.org/web/20050830063643/http://www.stanford.edu/dept/EIS/okin_conference/speakers. html#mackinno) 2005 Fellow of Stanford's Center for Advanced Study in the Behavioral Sciences

[7] Academic look at 'Deep Throat' (http://www.nytimes.com/2005/02/09/arts/09iht-Chuh.html) by Charles McGrath, 2005-02-09 alt URL (http://www.nytimes.com/2005/02/09/movies/09thro.html)

[8] 'Deep Throat': When Naughty Was Nice (http://www.washingtonpost.com/wp-dyn/articles/A12637-2005Feb9.html) by Tina Brown, 2005-02-10, alt URL (http://www.nysun.com/on-the-town/when-talk-was-deep/9054/)

[9] Is It Wrong To Pay For Sex? (http://www.npr.org/templates/story/story.php?storyId=103639465) 2009-04-29

[10] Catharine A. MacKinnon, Points Against Postmodernism, 75 *Chi.-Kent L. Rev.* 687, 687-88 (2000).

[11] "A Firebrand Flickers: The legendary feminist Catharine MacKinnon spurred the law to protect women, but the next wave is tired of feeling sheltered" (http://www.legalaffairs.org/issues/March-April-2006/review_Dinner_marapr06.msp). *Legal Affairs*. March 2006. . Retrieved 2007-07-27.

[12] Frances Olsen, Feminist Theory in Grand Style, 89 *Colum. L. Rev.* 1147, 1147 & n.4 (1989) (citing Conversation with Professor Nadine Taub, attorney with Rutgers Legal Clinic who litigated early sexual harassment cases (July 1985) and MacKinnon's book at page xi).

[13] http://www.mcolaw.com/docs/ao_tobreakthesilence_speech.pdf This essay contains the recollections of undergraduates who worked with MacKinnon on Alexander v. Yale, who recall her personal charisma and groundbreaking legal theory.

[14] Catharine A. MacKinnon, "The Logic of Experience: Reflections on the Development of Sexual Harassment Law," 90 *Geo. L.J.* 813, 824 (2002).

[15] Catharine A. MacKinnon, Pornography, Civil Rights, and Speech, 20 *Harv. C.R.-C.L. L. Rev.* 1 (1985). For support for her claim that snuff films exist, MacKinnon said in footnote 61, "In the movies known as snuff films, victims sometimes are actually murdered."' 130 Cong. Rec. S13192 (daily ed. Oct. 3, 1984)(statement of Senator Specter introducing the Pornography Victims Protection Act). Information on the subject is understandably hard to get. See People v. Douglas, Felony Complaint No. NF 8300382 (Municipal Court, Orange County, Cal. Aug. 5, 1983); "'Slain Teens Needed Jobs, Tried Porn'" and "Two Accused of Murder in 'Snuff' Films" Oakland Tribune, Aug. 6, 1983 (on file with Harvard Civil Rights-Civil Liberties Law Review); L. Smith, The Chicken Hawks (1975)(unpublished manuscript) (on file with Harvard Civil Rights-Civil Liberties Law Review).

[16] Dworkin, Ronald. "Women and Pornography", *New York Review of Books* 40, no. 17 (21 October 1993): 299. "...no reputable study has concluded that pornography is a significant cause of sexual crime: many of them conclude, on the contrary, that the causes of violent personality lie mainly in childhood"

[17] Malamuth, Neil M., and Joseph Ceniti. *Repeated Exposure to Violent and Nonviolent Pornography: Likelihood of Raping Ratings and Laboratory Aggression Against Women* (American Psychological Association) (http://www.apa.org/divisions/div46/articles/malamuth. pdf), as accessed Nov. 3, 2011.

[18] "Canada's Thought Police" (http://www.efc.ca/pages/wired-3.03.html). . Retrieved 2007-07-27.

[19] "Canadian Customs and Legal Approaches to Pornography" (http://www.nostatusquo.com/ACLU/dworkin/OrdinanceCanada.html). . Retrieved 2007-07-27.

[20] Catharine A. MacKinnon, *Toward a Feminist Theory of the State* (1989)

[21] Catharine A. MacKinnon, Pornography, Civil Rights, and Speech, 20 *Harv. C.R.-C.L. L. Rev.* 1, 3 & n.2 (1985)

[22] Fred R. Shapiro, "The Most-Cited Law Review Articles Revisited," 71 *Chi.-Kent L. Rev.* 751 (1996)

[23] Carol Vance, More Pleasure, More Danger: A Decade after the Barnard Sexuality Conference, in *Pleasure and Danger: Towards a Politics of Sexuality* (Carol Vance, ed., 1984).

[24] Catharine A. MacKinnon, *In Harm's Way* (1997).

[25] Catharine A. MacKinnon and Andrea Dworkin, Statement By Catharine A. Mackinnon and Andrea Dworkin regarding Canadian Customs and legal approaches to pornography (http://www.nostatusquo.com/ACLU/dworkin/OrdinanceCanada.html) (1994).

[26] "Oddest book titles prize shortlist announced" (http://www.thebookseller.com/news/53656-oddest-book-titles-prize-shortlist-announced. html). The Bookseller. 2008-02-22. . Retrieved 2008-02-24.

[27] http://www.bookfinder.com/author/catharine-a-mackinnon/

[28] http://www.bc.edu/bc_org/avp/cas/comm/free_speech/hudnut.html

[29] http://cyber.law.harvard.edu/vaw00/hudnut.html

[30] http://avalon.law.yale.edu/diana/4298-12.asp

[31] http://caselaw.lp.findlaw.com/cgi-bin/getcase.pl?court=2nd&navby=docket&no=949035

[32] http://avalon.law.yale.edu/diana/3junec.asp

External links

- Faculty biography at University of Michigan (http://cgi2.www.law.umich.edu/_FacultyBioPage/ facultybiopagenew.asp?ID=219) – includes bibliography of journal articles by MacKinnon
- MacKinnon expertise and contact info (http://www.ns.umich.edu/htdocs/public/experts/ExpDisplay. php?ExpID=497), University of Michigan
- A bibliography of MacKinnon's works (http://www.cddc.vt.edu/feminism/MacKinnon.html), 1999
- Biography on A&E (http://www.biography.com/articles/Catharine-Alice-MacKinnon-9393211)
- The *South China Morning Post* review of *Are Women Human?* (http://antonellagambottoburke.com/ NonfictionReviewHuman.htm)
- Marxism, Liberalism, and Feminism: Leftist Legal Thought (http://books.google.com/ books?id=GrjPEY6yQNgC&printsec=frontcover&dq=eric+engle&hl=de&ei=afDjTdbyIcjFswbB9YGTBg& sa=X&oi=book_result&ct=result&resnum=1&ved=0CDQQ6AEwAA#v=onepage&q&f=false), New Delhi, Serials (2010), Eric Engle.

Interviews

- "A Conversation With Catherine MacKinnon" (http://www.pbs.org/thinktank/transcript215.html) transcript of interview by Ben Wattenberg, *Think Tank*, July 7, 1995.
- "Clinton Scandal: A Feminist Issue?" (http://www.democracynow.org/1998/1/26/ clinton_scandal_a_feminist_issue), interview with Katha Pollitt, Linda Hirshman, and Catherine MacKinnon by Amy Goodman, *Democracy Now!*, January 26, 1998. (link to streaming RealAudio file)
- "Catharine A.MacKinnon: Women and Sexuality" (http://www.ffiles.net/episodes/MacKinnon.mp3), interview by Jackie Arsenuk and Deric Shannon, *The F-Files*, 2006. (MP3 audio file)

By MacKinnon

- "Women's Anti-discrimination Committee opens discussion on strengthening 'legal backbone' of women's convention with general recommendation on implementation" (http://www.un.org/News/Press/docs/2004/ wom1461.doc.htm), Press Release WOM/1461, United Nations Committee on Elimination of Discrimination against Women, July 21, 2004.

Criticism of MacKinnon

- "The Prime of Miss Kitty MacKinnon" (http://susiebright.blogs.com/Old_Static_Site_Files/ Prime_Of_Kitty_MacKinnon.pdf) by Susie Bright, *East Bay Express*, October 1993.
- "Catharine A. MacKinnon: The Rise of a Feminist Censor, 1983-1993" (http://www.mediacoalition.org/ reports/mackinnon.html) by Christopher M. Finan, *The Media Coalition*, November 1993.
- "Prof. MacKinnon an enemy of University's values" (http://www.michigandaily.com/content/ prof-mackinnon-enemy-universitys-values) editorial by Justin Shubow, *Michigan Daily*, November 25, 2002.

Misandry

Misandry (🔊 /mɪˈsændri/) is the hatred or dislike of men or boys. Misandry comes from Greek *misos* (μῖσος, "hatred") and *anēr*, *andros* (ἀνήρ, gen. ἀνδρός; "man"). *Misandry* is the antonym of philandry, the fondness towards men, love, or admiration of them. The term misogyny is the equivalent term for women.

In literature

Ancient Greek literature

Classics professor Froma Zeitlin of Princeton University discussed misandry in her article titled "Patterns of Gender in Aeschylean Drama: Seven against Thebes and the Danaid Trilogy."[1] She writes:

> The most significant point of contact, however, between Eteocles and the suppliant Danaids is, in fact, their extreme positions with regard to the opposite sex: the misogyny of Eteocles' outburst against all women of whatever variety (Se. 181-202) has its counterpart in the seeming misandry of the Danaids, who although opposed to their Egyptian cousins in particular (marriage with them is incestuous, they are violent men) often extend their objections to include the race of males as a whole and view their cause as a passionate contest between the sexes (cf. Su. 29, 393, 487, 818, 951).[1]

Literary criticism

In his book, *Gender and Judaism: The Transformation of Tradition*, Harry Brod, a Professor of Philosophy and Humanities in the Department of Philosophy and Religion at the University of Northern Iowa, writes:

> In the introduction to *The Great Comic Book Heroes*, Jules Feiffer writes that this is Superman's joke on the rest of us. Clark is Superman's vision of what other men are really like. We are scared, incompetent, and powerless, particularly around women. Though Feiffer took the joke good-naturedly, a more cynical response would see here the Kryptonian's misanthropy, his misandry embodied in Clark and his misogyny in his wish that Lois be enamored of Clark (much like Oberon takes out hostility toward Titania by having her fall in love with an ass in Shakespeare's *Midsummer-Night's Dream*).[2]

Julie M. Thompson, a feminist author, connects misandry with envy of men, in particular "penis envy," a term coined by Sigmund Freud in 1908, in his theory of female sexual development.[3]

Comparisons with other forms of bigotry

In 1999, masculist writer Warren Farrell compared the dehumanizing stereotyping of men to the dehumanization of the Vietnamese people as "gooks."[1]

> In the past quarter century, we exposed biases against other races and called it racism, and we exposed biases against women and called it sexism. Biases against men we call humor.
>
> —Warren Farrell, *Women Can't Hear What Men Don't Say*

Religious Studies professors Paul Nathanson and Katherine Young made similar comparisons in their 2001, three-book series *Beyond the Fall of Man*,[4] which treats misandry as a form of prejudice and discrimination that has become institutionalized in North American society.

In the 2007 book *International Encyclopedia of Men and Masculinities*, Marc A. Ouellette directly contrasted misandry and misogyny, arguing that "misandry lacks the systemic, transhistoric, institutionalized, and legislated antipathy of misogyny."[5] Anthropologist David D. Gilmore argues that while misogyny is a "near-universal phenomenon" there is no female equivalent to misogyny. He writes:

> Man hating among women has no popular name because it has never (at least not until recently) achieved apotheosis as a social *fact*, that is, it has never been ratified into public, culturally recognized and approved *institutions* (...) As a cultural institution, misogyny therefore seems to stand alone as a gender-based phobia, unreciprocated.[6]

Gilmore also states that neologisms like misandry refer "not to the hatred of men as men, but to the hatred of men's traditional male role" and a "culture of machismo". Therefore, he argues, misandry is "different from the intensely *ad feminam* aspect of misogyny that targets women no matter what they believe or do".[6]

Alleged instances

Academic Alice Echols, in her 1989 book *Daring To Be Bad: Radical Feminism in America, 1967–1975*, argued that radical feminist Valerie Solanas, best known for her attempted murder of Andy Warhol in 1968, displayed an extreme level of misandry compared to other radical feminists of the time in her tract, *The SCUM Manifesto*. Echols stated,

> Solanas's unabashed misandry—especially her belief in men's biological inferiority—her endorsement of relationships between 'independent women,' and her dismissal of sex as 'the refuge of the mindless' contravened the sort of radical feminism which prevailed in most women's groups across the country.[7]

Some other researchers have argued that Solanas' *SCUM Manifesto* was a parody of patriarchy and the Freudian theory of femininity, where the word *woman* was replaced by *man*. The text contains all the clichés of Freudian psychoanalytical theory: the biological accident, the incomplete sex and "penis envy" which became "pussy envy."[8][9] She was later diagnosed with paranoid schizophrenia and depression; some observers think she was suffering from these illnesses at the time of her writing.[10][11][12]

Nathanson and Young argued that "ideological feminism" has imposed misandry on culture.[13] Their 2001 book, *Spreading Misandry*, analyzed "pop cultural artifacts and productions from the 1990s" from movies to greeting cards for what they considered to be pervasive messages of hatred toward men. *Legalizing Misandry* (2005), the second in the series, gave similar attention to laws in North America.

In 2002, pundit Charlotte Hays wrote "that the anti-male philosophy of radical feminism has filtered into the culture at large is incontestable; indeed, this attitude has become so pervasive that we hardly notice it any longer".[14]

Wendy McElroy

Wendy McElroy, an individualist feminist and Fox News commentator,[15] wrote in 2001 that some feminists "have redefined the view of the movement of the opposite sex" as "a hot anger toward men seems to have turned into a cold hatred."[16] She argued it was a misandrist position to consider men, as a class, to be irreformable or rapists. McElroy stated "a new ideology has come to the forefront... radical or gender, feminism," one that has "joined hands with [the] political correctness movement that condemns the panorama of western civilization as sexist and racist: the product of 'dead white males'."[17]

As a criticism of feminism

In his 1997 book *The Gender Knot: Unraveling Our Patriarchal Legacy*, sociologist Allan G. Johnson stated that accusations of man-hating have been used to put down feminists. Johnson notes that the word *misandry* did not appear in dictionaries until recently, but the concept of the hatred of men is long established. The accusation of misandry is often effective against feminists because "people often confuse men as individuals with men as a dominant and privileged category of people."[18] He wrote that given the "reality of women's oppression, male privilege, and men's enforcement of both, it's hardly surprising that *every* woman should have moments where she resents or even hates 'men'."[18]

References

[1] Zeitlin, Froma I. (PDF). *Patterns of Gender in Aeschylean Drama: Seven against Thebes and the Danaid Trilogy* (http://repositories.cdlib. org/cgi/viewcontent.cgi?article=1008&context=ucbclassics). . Retrieved 2007-12-21. Princeton University, paper given at the Department of Classics, University of California, Berkeley

[2] *Gender and Judaism: The Transformation of Tradition* (http://books.google.com/books?hl=en&lr=&id=SH8r3ntJG8AC&oi=fnd& pg=PA279&dq=greek+misandry&ots=DIRliG6cvR&sig=RAkhjK9tDe9tKUt92TME85D7dL4), *Harry Brod*

[3] Emphasis added. Julie M. Thompson, *Mommy Queerest: Contemporary Rhetorics of Lesbian Maternal Identity*, (Amherst: University of Massachusetts Press, 2002).

[4] (Nathanson & Young 2001, pp. 4–6) "The same problem that long prevented mutual respect between Jews and Christians, the teaching of contempt, now prevents mutual respect between men and women."

[5] Flood, Michael, ed. (2007-07-18). *International Encyclopedia of Men and Masculinities* (http://books.google.com/ ?id=EUON2SYps-QC&pg=PA442&dq=michael+flood+misandry#v=onepage&q=michael flood misandry&f=false). *et al.*. London; New York: Routledge. ISBN 0-41533-343-1. .

[6] Gilmore, David G. "Misogyny: The Male Malady". Philadelphia: University of Pennsylvania Press, 2009, pp. 10-13, ISBN 978-0-81-221770-4.

[7] Echols, Nicole. "Daring to Be Bad: Radical Feminism in America, 1967-1975" (http://books.google.com/books?id=6zaVkAjBuPEC& pg=PA104). Minneapolis: University of Minnesota Press, 1989, pp. 104-105, ISBN 978-0-81-661786-9.

[8] Castro, Ginette. "American Feminism: A Contemporary History" (http://books.google.com/books?id=DYuBjJXGsZkC&pg=PA73). New York: New York University Press, 1990, p. 73, ISBN 978-0-81-471435-5.

[9] Smith, Patricia Juliana. "The Queer Sixties" (http://books.google.com/books?id=4bxltKXsftIC&pg=PA68). New York: Routledge, 1999, p. 68, ISBN 978-0-41-592168-8.

[10] Valerie Jean Solanas (1936-88) (http://books.guardian.co.uk/news/articles/0,,1432425,00.html) *The Guardian*

[11] Bockris, Victor. *Warhol: The Biography*. Da Capo Press (2003) ISBN 030681272X

[12] Harron and Minahan. *I Shot Andy Warhol*. Grove Press (1996) ISBN 0802134912

[13] (Nathanson & Young 2001, p. xiv) "[ideological feminism,] one form of feminism — one that has had a great deal of influence, whether directly or indirectly, on both popular culture and elite culture—is profoundly misandric".

[14] Hays, Charlotte. 'The Worse Half.' *National Review* 11 March 2002.

[15] The Independent Institute (http://www.independent.org/aboutus/person_detail.asp?id=488)

[16] (McElroy 2001, p. 5)

[17] (McElroy 2001, pp. 4–6)

[18] Johnson, Allan G. (2005). *The Gender Knot: Unraveling Our Patriarchal Legacy* (http://books.google.com/books?id=3nnxlqbN-IEC& pg=PA107). Temple University Press. p. 107. ISBN 1592133835. .

Further reading

- Summers, Christina Hoff (1995) [First published 1994]. *Who Stole Feminism: How Women Have Betrayed Women*. Simon & Schuster. ISBN 0-68480-156-8.
- Farrell, Warren (2001) [First published 1993]. *The Myth of Male Power: Why Men Are the Disposable Sex*. Berkley Trade. ISBN 0-425-18144-8.
- Ferguson, Frances; Bloch, R. Howard (1989). *Misogyny, Misandry, and Misanthropy*. Berkeley: University of California Press. ISBN 0-52006-546-8.
- Levine, Judith (1992). *My Enemy, My Love: Man-Hating and Ambivalence in Women's Lives*. Da Capo Press. ISBN 1-56025-568-4.
- McElroy, Wendy (2001). *Sexual Correctness: The Gender-Feminist Attack on Women*. Harper Paperbacks. New York: McFarland & Company. ISBN 0-78641-144-3
- Nathanson, Paul; Young, Katherine R. (2001). *Spreading Misandry: The Teaching of Contempt for Men in Popular Culture*. Harper Paperbacks. Montreal: McGill-Queen's University Press. ISBN 0-77353-099-7
- Nathanson, Paul; Young, Katherine R. (2006). *Legalizing Misandry: From Public Shame to Systemic Discrimination Against Men*. Montreal: McGill-Queen's University Press. ISBN 0-77352-862-8
- Schwartz, Howard (2003). *The Revolt of the Primitive: An Inquiry into the Roots of Political Correctness* (Revised ed.). Transaction Publishers. ISBN 0-76580-537-5.

External links

- Bailée, Susan; Sommers, Christina Hoff (2001). "Misandry in the Classroom". *The Hudson Review* (The Hudson Review, Inc.) **54** (1): 148–54. doi:10.2307/3852834. JSTOR 3852834. "My rough-and-tumble first grader, Mark, came home from school yesterday and nonchalantly told me a story about his day that set me shivering"
- Leader, Richard (2007). "Misandry: From the Dictionary of Fools" (http://adonismirror.com/ 10152006_leader_misandry_and_misanthropy.htm). *Adonis Mirror*. Retrieved 2007-12-28. article critical of the use of the term
- Wilson, Robert Anton (April 1996). "Androphobia: The only respectable bigotry" (http://www.backlash.com/ content/gender/1996/4-apr96/wilson04.html). *The Backlash!*. Shameless Men Press. Retrieved 2007-12-28.

Rosetta Reitz

Rosetta Reitz (September 28, 1924–November 1, 2008) was an American feminist and jazz historian who searched for and established a record label producing 18 albums of the music of the early women of jazz and the blues.[1]

Reitz was born in Utica, New York on September 28, 1924. She attended the University of Buffalo for one year and the University of Wisconsin–Madison for two years. After leaving college, she moved to Manhattan and worked at the Gotham Book Mart, later opening the Four Seasons, a bookstore in Greenwich Village she operated from 1947-1956.[2] Throughout her varied career she worked as a stockbroker, owner of a greeting card business, a college professor and a food columnist for *The Village Voice* and authored a book about mushrooms *Mushroom Cookery*,.[1]

Reitz was one of the second wave of feminism's earliest theory writers as author of the 1971 *The Village Voice* article "The Liberation of the Yiddishe Mama" and was a member of New York Radical Feminists and co-founder of the Older Women's Liberation (OWL).[2] She then wrote 1977 book *Menopause: A Positive Approach*, which was one of the first such books to have focused on menopause from the perspective of women, rather than with a medical approach.[1] While writing the book, she listened to her music recordings which told of the strength of women, not their role as victims.[1] Reitz noted that all the books she had read treated menopause as a dysfunction. She spent three years and spoke to 1,000 women in writing the book.[3]

Using $10,000 she borrowed from friends, Rosetta Records was established in 1979. She would search for lost music, most often from record collectors. The music that Reitz discovered was usually in the public domain, but she would try to determine if there were any current rights and ensure that royalties were paid to the artists.[1] Her music collections were built on old 78 rpm records of lesser-known performers including trumpeter and singer Valaida Snow, pianist-singer Georgia White, as well as others, such as Bessie Brown, Bertha Idaho and Maggie Jones. She also found long lost songs from better-known artists such as Ida Cox, Ma Rainey, Bessie Smith and Mae West. Her collecting covered the period from the 1920s to the 1960s, with particular attention to the Blues queens of the 1920s.[1][4]

She would remaster the recordings, research the background of the artists and write liner notes. She designed the graphics for album covers and included historic photographs. While early records were shipped by mail, ultimately there were more than ten stores that carried the Rosetta label. With changes in recording media, the label switched to tapes and later CDs. Though official sales figures were never disclosed, Reitz estimated that the four "independent women's blues" compilation albums each sold 20,000 copies. The last album released came in the mid-1990s, but older releases were available online and the artists she found had been picked up by a number of mainstream recording labels.[1]

Rosetta Reitz

Rosetta Reitz with the Performers of the Blues is a Woman Concert at the Newport Jazz Festival

Rosetta Reitz

In 1980 and 1981, Reitz organized a tribute to the "Women of Jazz" at Avery Fisher Hall as part of the Newport Jazz Festival. Called "The Blues is a Woman", the program, narrated by Carmen McRae, featured music by Adelaide Hall, Big Mama Thornton, Nell Carter and Koko Taylor.[5] Ms Reitz was the recipient of three awards—the Wonder Woman Award of 1982, a Grandmother Winifred grant in 1994, and the Veteran Feminists of America 2002 Roll of Honor for feminists writers.[2]

She died at age 84 on November 1, 2008 in Manhattan, New York of cardiopulmonary problems.[1] She is survived by 3 daughters and a granddaughter.

References

[1] Martin, Douglas. "Rosetta Reitz, Champion of Jazz Women, Dies at 84" (http://www.nytimes.com/2008/11/15/arts/music/15reitz. html), *The New York Times*, November 14, 2008. Accessed November 19, 2008.

[2] Reinholz, Mary. "Rosetta Reitz, 84, jazz historian, feminist writer", 'The Villager, *November 12-18, 2008.*

[3] Grossman, Ellie "Menopause Needn't Be Taboo: Time to Savor What You're Doing" (http://news.google.com/ newspapers?id=RBkLAAAAIBAJ&sjid=VFADAAAAIBAJ&pg=6877,939210&dq=menopause-a-positive-approach), *The Prescott Courier*, January 17, 1978. Accessed November 21, 2008.

[4] Sutro, Dirk. "Ladies Sing the Blues Rosetta Reitz single-handedly runs the only label devoted to keeping alive rare jazz and blues recordings by female artists" (http://pqasb.pqarchiver.com/latimes/access/61603416.html?dids=61603416:61603416&FMT=ABS& FMTS=ABS:FT&date=Apr+12,+1992&author=DIRK+SUTRO&pub=Los+Angeles+Times+(pre-1997+Fulltext)&desc=JAZZ+ Ladies+Sing+the+Blues+Rosetta+Reitz+single-handedly+runs+the+only+label+devoted+to+keeping+alive+rare+jazz+and+ blues+recordings+by+female+artists&pqatl=google), *Los Angeles Times*, April 12, 1992. Acecssed November 21, 2008.

[5] Swartley, Ariel. "LADIES SING THE BLUES; BLUES" (http://select.nytimes.com/gst/abstract. html?res=F40812FD345A12728DDDA00A94DE405B8084F1D3), *The New York Times*, June 29, 1980. Accessed November 21, 2008.

External links

- Rosetta Reitz Papers at Duke University (http://library.duke.edu/digitalcollections/rbmscl/reitzrosetta/inv/)
- Jazz Archive at Duke University (http://library.duke.edu/specialcollections/collections/jazzindex.html)
- Rosetta Records Liner Notes on Flickr (http://www.flickr.com/photos/47236461@N02/sets/ 72157623234176541/)

Florence Rush

Florence Rush (January 23, 1918—December 9, 2008) was an American certified social worker (M.S.W. from the University of Pennsylvania[1]), feminist theorist and organizer best known for introducing The Freudian Coverup in her presentation "The Sexual Abuse of Children: A Feminist Point of View" about childhood sexual abuse and incest at the April 1971 New York Radical Feminists (NYRF) Rape Conference [2] Rush's paper at the time was the first challenge to Freudian theories of children as the seducers of adults rather than the victims of adults' sexual/power exploitation.[3]

Rush observed the problem of childhood sexual abuse as a psychiatric social worker at the New York Society for the Prevention of Cruelty to Children[4] and at a facility for delinquent female adolescents, although at the time—during the 1950s and 1960s—such therapists were instructed to avoid discussing incest with their young patients because of prevailing Freudian theories.[5]

Rush's NYRF Rape Conference presentation about incest and childhood sexual abuse reviewed psychiatric and psychoanalytical literature from Freud to that time that attributed such problems to children's seduction of adults or erotic fantasies. She then linked these prevailing psychiatric theories about the child's instigation of or erotic fantasies about incest and sexual abuse to maintaining a climate for the political and psychological oppression of women. As Rush concluded in her presentation the "sexual abuse of children..is an unspoken but prominent factor in socializing and preparing the female to accept a subordinate role: to feel guilty, ashamed, and to tolerate through fear, the power exercised over her by men" [6][7]

Rush subsequently authored the 1977 *Freud and the Sexual Abuse of Children* in the first volume of a feminist theory journal, *Chyrsalis*,[8] and the 1980 Prentice Hall *The Best Kept Secret: The Sexual Abuse of Children* that additionally traced the toleration of sexual abuse of children to the beginnings of history. Her continued work to counter sexual abuse of women and children and the media imagery feminists believe propagates such abuse encompassed key roles in many organizations. She served as 1979 co-founder and 1979-1987 lecturer for Women Against Pornography, 1980–1985 chair of the National Organization of Women (NOW)'s New York City Chapter's Media Reform Committee, Board of Directors Member of New York Women Against Rape where she produced and exhibited a slide presentation on the increasing media eroticism of children, and member of the New York State Psychiatric Institute's Advisory Committee on the Treatment of Sexual Aggressors.[6]

Rush was an early participant in the second wave of U.S. feminism when, in 1970, she became co-founder and steering committee member of Older Women's Liberation (OWL).[1] She was to conclude her feminist work between 2002 and 2005 as chair of New York City NOW's Older Women's Committee where she organized against Republican presidential and congressional efforts to reduce budget deficits by reigning in Social Security and Medicare benefit costs.[6]

Rush was also concerned about women's role definitions and expectations within families as author of *Women in the Middle*, the first article about sandwich generation women taking care of both children and elderly relatives, published in *Notes from the Third Year* and *Radical Feminism*[9][10] In the mid-1970s she produced and exhibited a slide show presentation "From Mother Goddess to Father Knows Best" about the depreciation of mothers from ancient mythology to 20th century media representations.[11] As a mother struggling with the role of caretaker to her son, Matthew, and his lover, Ron, when they became ill with AIDS in 1987, Rush's organizing around feminist issues extended to mothers of AIDS patients as an active participant in a mothers' support group of the People With AIDS Coalition of New York [12] After Matthew and Ron died in 1990, she founded and participated in the first Bereavement Group for such mothers.[11]

Rush was born to Russian immigrants in Manhattan and grew up in the Bronx, NY before moving to New Rochelle, NY. She subsequently moved to Manhattan's Greenwich Village in the early 1970s. She was married to Bernard Rush and is survived by son, Thomas, his two children, and daughter, Eleanor.[3] In 2005, she was honored with the New York City NOW's Chapter Susan B. Anthony Award to grassroots feminists.[6]

References

[1] Love, Barbara J. and Nancy F. Cott. *Feminists Who Changed America, 1963—1975.* University of Illinois Press, 2008 p. 399

[2] Connell, Noreen and Wilson, Casandra, eds. *Rape: The First Sourcebook for Women by New York Radical Feminists* New American Library, 1974 p. 65

[3] Obituary "Florence Rush, 90, feminist author who focused on child abuse", *The Villager*, December 24–30, 2008.

[4] Kamienski, Laura Ann *Women's Self Defense* Internet essay, accessed January 22, 2009

[5] Hallen-Pleck, Elizabeth, *Domestic Tyranny, The Making of American Social Policy Against Family Violence from Colonial Times to the Present.* University of Illinois Press, 2004 p. 155

[6] Connell, Noreen, February 24, 2005 New York National Organization for Women Susan B. Anthony Awards ceremony presentation.

[7] Doane, Janice L. and Hodges, Devon L. *Telling Incest.* University of Michigan Press, 2001 p. 50

[8] Braude, Marjorie, *Women, Power and Therapy.* Hawthorne Press, 1987 p. 64

[9] Gould, Jane, *Juggling.* Feminist Press, 1997 p.154

[10] Koedt, Anne, Ellen Levine, and Anita Rapone, eds. *Radical Feminism.* Quadrangle/New York Times Book Company, 1973

[11] Rich, Nicole, "From Suburban Housewife to Radical Feminist" in Chesler, Phyllis, Rothblum, Esther, Cole, Ellen eds. *Feminist Foremothers in Women's Studies.* Hawthorne Press, 1996 pp.419-425

[12] Dullea, Georgia, "AIDS Mothers' Undying Hope", *New York Times*, April 20, 1994 accessed January 25, 2009

Valerie Solanas

Valerie Solanas	
Solanas at the *Village Voice* offices, February 1967	
Born	Valerie Jean Solanas April 9, 1936 Ventnor City, New Jersey, US
Died	April 25, 1988 (aged 52) San Francisco, California, US
Occupation	Writer
Nationality	American
Subjects	Feminism
Literary movement	Feminist movement
Notable work(s)	*SCUM Manifesto* (1968)
Children	Possibly a son

Valerie Jean Solanas (April 9, 1936 – April 25, 1988) was an American radical feminist writer, best known for her attempted murder of Andy Warhol in 1968. She wrote the *SCUM Manifesto*, which called for male gendercide and the creation of an all-female society.

Early life

Solanas was born in Ventnor City, New Jersey, to Louis Solanas and Dorothy Biondi (or Moran), in 1936.[1][2] Her father was a bartender and her mother, a dental assistant or a nurse.[1][3] She had a younger sister, Judith A. Solanas Martinez.[4]

Valerie Solanas claimed she regularly suffered sexual abuse at the hands of her father.[3] Her parents divorced when she was 11, and her mother remarried shortly afterwards. Solanas disliked her stepfather and began rebelling against her mother, becoming a truant. As a child, she would write insults for children to use on one another, for the cost of a dime. She beat up a boy in high school who was bothering a younger girl, and also hit a nun.[1] Because of her rebellious behavior, her mother sent her to be raised by her grandfather in 1949. Solanas claimed her grandfather was a violent alcoholic who often beat her. When she was 15, she left her grandfather and became homeless.[5] Between 1951[6] and 1953, she gave birth to a son, fathered by a married man or a sailor.[6][7] The child, named David (later, David Blackwell, by adoption), was taken away from Solanas and she never saw him again.[6][8][9][10]

In spite of this, she graduated from high school on time and earned a degree in psychology from the University of Maryland, College Park, where she was in the Psi Chi Honor Society.[11][12] While at the University of Maryland, she hosted a call-in radio show where she gave advice on how to combat men.[3]

She did nearly a year at the University of Minnesota's Graduate School of Psychology, where she published two articles, and worked in the psychology department's animal research laboratory,[13] before dropping out and moving to attend Berkeley for a few courses, when she began writing the *SCUM Manifesto*.[14]

New York City and The Factory

In the mid 1960s Solanas moved to New York City where she supported herself through begging and prostitution.[15][11] In 1965 she wrote two works: a short story called "A Young Girl's Primer, or How to Attain the Leisure Class", and a play titled *Up Your Ass*[16] about a man-hating prostitute and a panhandler. The short story was published in *Cavalier* magazine in 1966.[17]

In 1967, Solanas encountered Andy Warhol outside his studio, The Factory, and asked him to produce her play. He accepted the script for review and told Solanas that it was "well typed" and promised to read it.[18] According to Factory lore, Warhol, whose films were often shut down by the police for obscenity, thought the script was so pornographic that it must be a police trap.[19][20] Solanas contacted Warhol about the script, and was told that he had lost it. He also jokingly offered her a job at the Factory as a typist. Insulted, Solanas demanded money for the lost manuscript. Instead, Warhol paid her $25 to appear in his film, *I, A Man*.[18] In his book, *Popism: The Warhol Sixties*, Warhol wrote that before she shot him, he thought Solanas was an interesting and funny person, but that her constant demands for attention made her difficult to deal with and ultimately drove him away.

In her role in *I, A Man*, she and the film's title character (played by Tom Baker) haggle in a building hallway over whether they should go into her apartment. Solanas dominates the improvised conversation, leading Baker through a dialogue about everything from "squishy asses", "men's tits", and lesbian "instinct". Ultimately, she leaves him to fend for himself, explaining "I gotta go beat my meat" as she exits the scene. Solanas was satisfied with her experience working with Warhol and her performance in the film, and brought Maurice Girodias to see the film. Girodias described her as being "very relaxed and friendly with Warhol." Solanas also had a nonspeaking role in Warhol's film *Bikeboy*, in 1967.[20]

In 1967, Solanas self-published her best-known work, the *SCUM Manifesto*, a scathing, misandric attack on the male sex. "SCUM", generally held to be an acronym of "Society for Cutting Up Men", actually does not appear as an acronym in the body of the manifesto. Its opening words refer immediately to its directives:

> "Life" in this "society" being, at best, an utter bore and no aspect of "society" being at all relevant to women, there remains to civic-minded, responsible, thrill-seeking females only to overthrow the government, eliminate the money system, institute complete automation and eliminate the male sex. [¶] It's now technically possible to reproduce without the aid of males (or, for that matter, females) and to produce only females. We must begin immediately to do so. The male is a biological accident ....
>
> —Valerie Solanas, SCUM Manifesto

[21]

The *SCUM Manifesto* would be published by Olympia Press in 1968, a publishing house owned by Girodias. In the contract, Girodias requested that Solanas "give me your next writing, and other writings," after he gave her $500. She took this to mean that Girodias would own her work. She told Paul Morrissey that "everything I write will be his. He's done this to me, he's screwed me!" Solanas intended to write a novel based around the *SCUM Manifesto*, and believed that a conspiracy was behind Warhol not returning the *Up Your Ass* script, believing that he was coordinating with Girodias to steal her work and use it themselves. That spring, Solanas went to writer Paul Krassner for money, telling him that she intended to shoot Girodias. Krassner gave her $50 and she purchased a .32 automatic pistol.[22]

The shooting

On June 3, 1968, at 9:00 a.m., Solanas arrived at the Chelsea Hotel where Girodias lived. She asked the front desk for him, and was told he was gone for the weekend. She remained at the hotel for three hours before visiting the office of Grove Press, where she asked for Barney Rosset, who was not there.[23] Around noon[23] Solanas arrived at The Factory and waited for Warhol outside.[24] Morrissey arrived and asked her what she was doing there, and she replied "I'm waiting for Andy to get money". Morrissey tried to get rid of her, telling her that Warhol wasn't coming in that day, but she replied by telling him she'd wait. At 2:00 p.m. she went up into the studio, and Morrissey persisted in telling her that Warhol was not coming in and that she had to leave. She left, then traveled up and down the elevator seven more times before making a final trip with Warhol.[23]

She entered the Factory with Warhol and he complimented her on her look. Solanas had worn a black turtleneck sweater and a raincoat, styled her hair, and wore lipstick and makeup, contradictory to her usual butch look. Morrissey told her to leave, and threatened to "beat the hell" out of her and throw her out if she did not go. The phone rang and Warhol took the call as Morrissey went to the bathroom. While he was on the phone, Solanas shot at him three times. The first two shots missed, and the third went through his left lung, spleen, stomach, liver, esophagus and finally his right lung.[23] She then shot art critic Mario Amaya, shooting him in the right hip, and tried to shoot Warhol's manager Fred Hughes by shooting him in the head point blank, but her gun jammed.[24] Hughes asked her to leave, which she did, leaving behind a paper bag with her address book on a table.[24] Warhol, declared clinically dead, was taken to Columbus Hospital, and operated on by five doctors for five hours, who saved his life.[23]

Later that day, Solanas turned herself in to Officer William Schmalix, a passing NYPD officer; she produced the gun and told him about the shooting. She was fingerprinted and charged with felonious assault and possession of a deadly weapon.[25] The morning after, the *New York Daily* ran the front page headline "Actress Shoots Andy Warhol." Solanas proceeded to request a correction, and later that evening the headline was changed. An updated caption read a quote from Solanas stating "I'm a writer, not an actress." Her demand to be called a writer helped to solidify her independence from Warhol, whom she stated, upon her arrest to the officer, "had too much control in my life."[26] After going into police custody, Solanas was brought before the Manhattan Criminal Court where she told the judge, "It's not often that I shoot someone. I didn't do it for nothing. Warhol had tied me up, lock, stock and barrel. He was going to do something to me which would have ruined me." She told the judge she would represent herself and she declared that she was "right in what I did! I have nothing to regret!" The judge would strike her comments from the record and send her to Bellevue Hospital for psychiatric observation.[25]

Trial

I consider that a moral act. And I consider it immoral that I missed. I should have done target practice.
--Valerie Solanas on her assassination attempt on Andy Warhol.[27]

Solanas appeared at the New York Supreme Court on June 13, 1968. Florynce Kennedy represented her and asked for a writ of habeas corpus, arguing that Solanas was being held inappropriately at Bellevue. The judge denied the motion and Solanas returned to Bellevue's psychiatric ward. On June 28, Solanas was indicted on charges of attempted murder, assault, and illegal possession of a gun. She was declared "incompetent" in August and sent to Wards Island to be hospitalized. That same month, Olympia Press published the *SCUM Manifesto* with essays by Girodias and Krassner.[25]

A year later, in June 1969, Solanas was deemed fit to stand trial. She represented herself without an attorney and pleaded guilty to "reckless assault with intent to harm".[28][29] She was sentenced to three years in prison, with the year she spent in a psychiatric ward counted as time served.[28][29]

After murder attempt

According to Robert Marmorstein in 1968, "[s]he has dedicated the remainder of her life to the avowed purpose of eliminating every single male from the face of the earth."[30] Feminist Robin Morgan (later editor of *Ms.* magazine) demonstrated for Solanas's release from prison. Ti-Grace Atkinson, the New York chapter president of the National Organization for Women (NOW), described Solanas as "the first outstanding champion of women's rights"[13][31] and as "a 'heroine' of the feminist movement",[32][33] and "smuggled [her manifesto] ... out of the mental hospital where Solanas was confined."[32][33] Another NOW member, Florynce Kennedy, called her "one of the most important spokeswomen of the feminist movement."[18][31] Norman Mailer called her the "Robespierre of feminism."[13]

In 2009, Margo Feiden, a former Broadway producer and playwright, said she was visited by Solanas on the morning of the shooting. According to interviews with *The New York Times* and *Interview* magazine, Solanas gave Feiden a play titled *The Society for Cutting Up Men*. Solanas tried to persuade Feiden to produce the play, but Feiden refused.[19] According to Feiden, Solanas warned that if Feiden would not produce the play, she would shoot Andy Warhol "as a publicity stunt to be famous, so that I would produce her play." Solanas threatened: "I'm going right now to shoot him. I want you to keep the play—that's what's in here (handing Feiden a worn green folder)."[34] Feiden said that she desperately tried to avert the shooting. She first called her cousin, Bob Feiden, who was a close friend of Warhol's; Feiden's secretary at Columbia Records said that he was out. Margo Feiden frantically continued to call the authorities: her local police station in Brooklyn, the police precinct that covered Warhol's address in Union Square, police headquarters (in SoHo), and Mayor Lindsay's office—but nobody took her calls seriously.[35]

Solanas & Warhol

After Solanas was released from the New York State Prison for Women in 1971,[36] she stalked Warhol and others over the telephone, and was arrested again. Solanas drifted into obscurity and was in and out of mental hospitals.

The attack had a profound impact on Warhol and his art, and The Factory scene became much more tightly controlled afterward. For the rest of his life, Warhol lived in fear that Solanas would attack him again. "It was the Cardboard Andy, not the Andy I could love and play with," said close friend and collaborator Billy Name. "He was so sensitized you couldn't put your hand on him without him jumping. I couldn't even love him anymore, because it hurt him to touch him."[37] While his friends were actively hostile towards Solanas, Warhol himself preferred not to discuss her.

Later life

Solanas may have intended to author an eponymous autobiography.[38] She did announce a book with her name as the title.[39]

Ultra Violet, according to her somewhat unreliable report,[40] interviewed her. Solanas was then known as Onz Loh. Solanas stated that the August 1968 version of the manifesto had many errors, unlike her own printed version of October 1967, and that the book had not sold well. She also said that until told by Ultra, she was unaware of Andy Warhol's death.[41]

Death and after

On April 25, 1988, at the age of 52, Solanas died of pneumonia at the Hotel Bristol in the Tenderloin district of San Francisco.[42] A building superintendent at the hotel, not on duty that night, "had a vague memory of Valerie [Solanas]. Once, ... he saw her typing at her desk. There was a pile of typewritten pages beside her. What she was writing and what happened to the manuscript remain a mystery."[43][6] Her mother burned all her belongings posthumously.[6]

Solanas died in 1988 of pneumonia at the Bristol Hotel in San Francisco.

Legacy

Popular culture

Valerie Solanas's life has been the focus of numerous performance, film, music and publications. In 1996 actress Lili Taylor played Solanas in the film *I Shot Andy Warhol*. The film focused on Solanas's assassination attempt on Warhol, and Taylor won Special Recognition for Outstanding Performance at the Sundance Film Festival for her role.[44] The film's director, Mary Harron, requested to use songs by the Velvet Underground, but was denied by Lou Reed, who feared that Solanas would be glorified in the film. Six years before the film's release, Reed would release the song "I Believe" about Solanas, where he sings: "I believe life's serious enough for retribution... I believe being sick is no excuse. And I believe I would've pulled the switch on her myself." Reed believed Solanas was to blame for Warhol's death from a gallbladder infection 20 years after she shot him.[45]

Three plays have been based around Solanas life. *Valerie Shoots Andy* by Carson Kreitzer from 2001, which starred two actresses playing a younger (Heather Grayson) and an older (Lynne McCollough) Solanas.[46] 2003's *Tragedy in Nine Lives*, by Karen Houppert, examined the encounter between Solanas and Warhol as a Greek tragedy and starred Juliana Francis as Solanas.[47] Most recently, in 2011, was *Pop!*, a musical by Maggie-Kate Coleman and Anna K. Jacobs. *Pop!* focused mainly on Andy Warhol, with Rachel Zampelli playing Solanas and singing the song "Big Gun", which was described as the "evening's strongest number" by *The Washington Post*.[48]

In 1999 *Up Your Ass* was re-discovered and produced in 2000 by George Coates Performance Works in San Francisco. Coates turned the piece into a musical, starring an all-female cast. Coates learned about *Up Your Ass* while at an exhibition at the Andy Warhol Museum, which marked the 30th anniversary of the shooting. The copy that Warhol had lost was discovered buried in a trunk of lighting equipment that was owned by Billy Name. Coates would consult with Solanas's sister, Judith, while writing the piece, and sought to create a "very funny satirist" out of Solanas, not just showing her as the attempted assassin of Warhol.[6] [47]

Swedish author Sara Stridsberg wrote a semi-fictional novel about Valerie Solanas, called *Drömfakulteten* (English: *The Dream Faculty*). In the book, the author visits Solanas towards the end of her life at the Bristol Hotel. Stridsberg was awarded The Nordic Council's Literature Prize for the book.[49]

Composer Pauline Oliveros released a piece titled "To Valerie Solanas and Marilyn Monroe in Recognition of Their Desperation" in 1970. Through the work, Oliveros sought to explore how "Both women seemed to be desperate and caught in the traps of inequality: Monroe needed to be recognized for her talent as an actress. Solanas wished to be supported for her own creative work."[50][51] There is a music group from Belgian called The Valerie Solanas.[52]

Influence and analysis

Valerie Solanas solidifed her role as a cult figure with the publication of the *SCUM Manifesto* and her shooting of Andy Warhol. James Martin Harding, in *Cutting Performances*, explains that by declaring herself independent from Andy Warhol, after her arrest she became a symbol of "avant-garde's rejection of the traditional structures of bourgeois theater," and explained that her anti-patriarchal attitude and actions pushed "avant-garde in radically new directions." Harding believes that Solanas's assassination attempt on Warhol was its own theatrical performance. At the shooting she left behind a paper bag in which she carried her gun. She left the bag on a countertop at the Factory, and it also held her address book and a sanitary napkin. Harding states that leaving behind the sanitary napkin was part of the performance, and calls "attention to basic feminine experiences that were publicly taboo and tacitly elided within avant-garde circles."[53]

Feminist philosopher Avital Ronell compares Solanas to an array of people: Lorena Bobbitt, a "girl Nietzsche, Medusa, the Unabomber, and Medea. Ronell believes that Solanas was threatened by the hyper-feminine women of the Factory that Warhol liked and felt lonely because of the rejection she felt due to her own butch androgyny. She believed that Solanas was ahead of her time, living in a period before feminist and lesbian revolutionaries such as the Guerilla Girls and the Lesbian Avengers.[13] Solanas has also been credited as instigating radical feminism[27], and Catherine Lord writes that "The feminist movement would not have happened without Valerie Solanas."[1] Lord believes that the reissuing of the *SCUM Manifesto* and the disowning of Solanas by "women's liberation politicos" triggered a wave of radical feminist publications. As women's liberation activists denied hating men, Vivian Gornick claimed that a year later the same women would change their stories, developing the first wave of radical feminism.[1]

However, writer Breanne Fahs describes Solanas as a contradiction which "alienates her from the feminist movement." These contradictions are seen in her lifestyle (a lesbian who sexually serviced men, claim of being asexual, confusion), a rejection of queer culture, and a disinterest in working with others despite a co-dependency on others. Fahs also brings into question the honesty of Solanas life. Solanas's life is described as one of a victim, a rebel, a desperate loner, yet Solanas's cousin says she worked as a waitress in her late 20s and 30s, not primarily as a prostitute, and friend Geoffrey LaGear said she had a "groovy childhood." Solanas also kept in touch with her father throughout her life, which makes one question if reconciliation took place regarding sexual abuse (or if such abuse happened). Fahs believes that Solanas used dramatic tales to sell her manifesto and popularize herself.[]

Notes

[1] Lord, Catherine (2010). "Wonder Waif Meets Super Neuter." (http://proxygw.wrlc.org/login?url=http://search.ebscohost.com/login. aspx?direct=true&db=aph&AN=50987036&site=ehost-live). *October (journal)* (132): 135-136. . Retrieved 27 November 2011.(subscription required)
[2] On "Moran": Ronell, Avital, *Deviant Payback: The Aims of Valerie Solanas*, as introduction in Solanas, Valerie, *SCUM Manifesto* (London: Verso, New ed. 2004 (ISBN 1-85984-553-3)), p. 31 n. 27, citing Gaither, Rowan, *Andy Warhol's Feminist Nightmare*, in *New York Magazine*, Jan. 14, 1991, p. 35 (author Avital Ronell prof. German & comparative lit. & chair German dep't, N.Y. Univ.).
[3] Watson, Steven (2003). *Factory made: Warhol and the sixties* (1st ed.). New York: Pantheon Books. pp. 35–36. ISBN 0679423729.
[4] Jansen, Sharon L., *Reading Women's Worlds from Christine de Pizan to Doris Lessing: A Guide to Six Centuries of Women Writers Imagining Rooms of Their Own* (N.Y.: Palgrave Macmillan, 1st ed. Apr., 2011 (ISBN 978-0-230-11066-3)), p. 141 (author a teacher).
[5] Buchanan, Paul D.. *Radical Feminists: A Guide to an American Subculture*. Santa Barbara, Calif.: Greenwood. p. 132. ISBN 1598843567.
[6] Judith Coburn (2000). "Solanas Lost and Found" (http://www.villagevoice.com/2000-01-11/news/solanas-lost-and-found/). Village Voice. . Retrieved 27 November 2011.
[7] Solanas's cousin claims the man was a sailor, and that Solanas may have also gave birth to a second child before leaving home.
[8] Jobey, Liz, *Solanas and Son, op. cit.*
[9] Hewitt, Nancy A., *Solanas, Valerie.*, in Ware, Susan, ed., & Stacy Lorraine Braukman, asst. ed., *Notable American Women: A Biographical Dictionary Completing the Twentieth Century* (Cambridge, Mass.: Belknap Press (Harvard Univ. Press), 2004 (ISBN 0-674-01488-X)), p. 602 (prep. under Radcliffe Institute for Advanced Study, Harvard Univ.).
[10] Lord states that Solanas and her son lived with "a middle-class military couple outside of Washington, D.C." before she went to the University of Maryland. This couple might have paid for her college tuition, according to Lord.
[11] Victoria Hesford; Lisa Diedrich (28 February 2010). *Feminist Time Against Nation Time: Gender, Politics, and the Nation-State in an Age of Permanent War* (http://books.google.com/books?id=Y4KHFSSEZ2gC&pg=PA154). Rowman & Littlefield. p. 154. ISBN 978-0-7391-4428-2. . Retrieved 25 November 2011.
[12] Regarding the honor society: Jansen, Sharon L., *Reading Women's Worlds from Christine de Pizan to Doris Lessing, op. cit.*, p. 152.
[13] Thom Nickels (1 November 2005). *Out In History: Collected Essays* (http://books.google.com/books?id=7NIjDI9uiEEC&pg=PA15). STARbooks Press. p. 17. ISBN 978-1-891855-58-0. . Retrieved 27 November 2011.
[14] Jobey, Liz, *Solanas and Son*, in *The Guardian* (London, England), Aug. 24, 1996, p. 10 (newspaper).
[15] Neil A. Hamilton (2002). *Rebels and renegades: a chronology of social and political dissent in the United States* (http://books.google. com/books?id=jZymqT1HmqAC&pg=PA264). Taylor & Francis. pp. 264–. ISBN 978-0-415-93639-2. . Retrieved 25 November 2011.
[16] The original title of the work is *Up Your Ass or From the Cradle to the Boat or The Big Suck or Up from the Slime.*Fahs, Breanne (2008). "The Radical Possibilities Of Valerie Solanas." (http://proxygw.wrlc.org/login?url=http://search.ebscohost.com/login. aspx?direct=true&db=aph&AN=36546443&site=ehost-live). *Feminist Studies 3* (34): 591-617. . Retrieved 27 November 2011.(subscription required)
[17] Watson, Steven (2003). *Factory Made: Warhol and the Sixties* (1st ed. ed.). New York: Pantheon Books. p. 447. ISBN 0679423729.
[18] Thom Nickels (1 November 2005). *Out In History: Collected Essays* (http://books.google.com/books?id=7NIjDI9uiEEC&pg=PA15). STARbooks Press. pp. 15–16. ISBN 978-1-891855-58-0. . Retrieved 27 November 2011.

[19] Barron, James (June 23, 2009). *A Manuscript, a Confrontation, a Shooting* (http://cityroom.blogs.nytimes.com/2009/06/23/a-manuscript-a-confrontation-a-shooting/), New York Times, retrieved on 2009-07-06

[20] Alan Kaufman; Barney Rosset (29 December 2004). *The outlaw bible of American literature* (http://books.google.com/books?id=knRlbjOR-lEC&pg=PA204). Basic Books. p. 201. ISBN 978-1-56025-550-5. . Retrieved 27 November 2011.

[21] Solanas, Valerie, *SCUM Manifesto* (Valerie Solanas, 1967), p. [1] (self-published) (copy from Northwestern University).

[22] Alan Kaufman; Barney Rosset (29 December 2004). *The outlaw bible of American literature* (http://books.google.com/books?id=knRlbjOR-lEC&pg=PA204). Basic Books. p. 202. ISBN 978-1-56025-550-5. . Retrieved 27 November 2011.

[23] Alan Kaufman; Barney Rosset (29 December 2004). *The outlaw bible of American literature* (http://books.google.com/books?id=knRlbjOR-lEC&pg=PA204). Basic Books. pp. 202–203. ISBN 978-1-56025-550-5. . Retrieved 27 November 2011.

[24] James Martin Harding (25 February 2010). *Cutting performances: collage events, feminist artists, and the American avant-garde* (http://books.google.com/books?id=IX8kznQvH54C&pg=PA151). University of Michigan Press. pp. 151–173. ISBN 978-0-472-11718-5. . Retrieved 27 November 2011.

[25] Alan Kaufman; Barney Rosset (29 December 2004). *The outlaw bible of American literature* (http://books.google.com/books?id=knRlbjOR-lEC&pg=PA204). Basic Books. p. 204. ISBN 978-1-56025-550-5. . Retrieved 27 November 2011.

[26] James Martin Harding (25 February 2010). *Cutting performances: collage events, feminist artists, and the American avant-garde* (http://books.google.com/books?id=IX8kznQvH54C&pg=PA151). University of Michigan Press. p. 152. ISBN 978-0-472-11718-5. . Retrieved 27 November 2011.

[27] Third, Amanda (2006). "Shooting From the Hip': Valerie Solanas, SCUM and the Apocalyptic Politics of Radical Feminism." (http://web.ebscohost.com.proxygw.wrlc.org/ehost/pdfviewer/pdfviewer?vid=6&hid=11&sid=f7484682-69ce-49ca-ae49-81707f709e76@sessionmgr4). *Hecate (journal)* **2** (32): 104-132. . Retrieved 27 November 2011.(subscription required)

[28] Jansen, Sharon L.. *Reading women's worlds from Christine de Pizan to Doris Lessing* (1st ed.). New York: Palgrave Macmillan. p. 153. ISBN 0230110665.

[29] Solanas, Valerie (1996). *SCUM manifesto*. San Francisco, CA: AK Press. p. 55. ISBN 1873176449.

[30] Marmorstein, Robert, *A Winter Memory Of Valerie Solanis [sic]: Scum Goddess*, in *The Village Voice* (New York, N.Y.), vol. XIII, no. 35, Thursday, Jun. 13, 1968, p. 9, col. 2 (unclear which is title and which subtitle, the longer & lower repeated on both continuation pp. & the shorter & higher not) (title in table of contents *The Woman Who Shot Andy Warhol—A Winter Memory of Valerie Solanis* (sic), per p. 2 (*In The Voice This Week*)).

[31] Solanas, Valerie (August 1996). *SCUM Manifesto*. AK Press. p. 54. ISBN 1-873176-44-9.

[32] Friedan, Betty, *It Changed My Life: Writings on the Women's Movement* (N.Y.: Random House, 1st ed. 1976 (© 1963–1964, 1966, & 1970–1976) (ISBN 0-394-46398-6)), p. 109 (in unnumbered chap. *"Our Revolution Is Unique": Excerpt from the President's Report to NOW, 1968*, in pt. II, *The Actions: Organizing the Women's Movement for Equality*) (author founder & 1st pres., NOW, & visiting prof. sociology, Temple Univ., Yale, New Sch. for Social Research, & Queens Coll.).

[33] Friedan, Betty, *"It Changed My Life": Writings on the Women's Movement* (Cambridge, Mass.: Harvard Univ. Press, 1st Harvard Univ. Press pbk. ed. 1998 (© 1963–1964, 1966, 1970–1976, 1985, 1991, & 1998) (ISBN 0-674-46885-6)), p. 138 (in unnumbered chap. *"Our Revolution Is Unique": Excerpt from the President's Report to NOW, 1968*, in pt. II, *The Actions: Organizing the Women's Movement for Equality*) (author founder & 1st pres., National Organization for Women, convener National Women's Political Caucus & National Abortion Rights Action League, & distinguished visiting prof., Cornell).

[34] O'Brien, Glenn. *History Rewrite* (http://www.interviewmagazine.com/culture/history-rewrite/), *Interview* magazine, retrieved on 2009-07-06

[35] Q: The Podcast for Monday July 6, 2009 (http://podcast.cbc.ca/mp3/qpodcast_20090706.mp3), Jian Ghomeshi interviews Margo Feiden, CBC Radio

[36] Buchanan, Paul D.. *Radical feminists: a guide to an American subculture*. Santa Barbara, Calif.: Greenwood. p. 48. ISBN 1598843567.

[37] Making the Scene: Factory Made: Warhol and the Sixties by Steven Watson (http://www.factorymade.org/fm/reviews.html), Dennis Drabelle, *Washington Post* book review, November 16, 2003.

[38] Winkiel, Laura, *The "Sweet Assassin" and the Performative Politics of SCUM Manifesto*, in Smith, Patricia Juliana, ed., *The Queer Sixties* (N.Y.: Routledge, 1999 (ISBN 0-415-92169-4)), p. 74 & n. 24 ("SCUM Manifesto" italicized in original title where balance of title not) (author, Ph.D. from Dep't of Eng., Univ. of Notre Dame, was research fellow, Ctr. for the Humanities, Wesleyan Univ., & ed. postdoctoral lecturer Eng. & teacher 20th cent. British lit. & gay/lesbian studies, Univ. of Calif., Los Angeles).

[39] Smith, Howard, & Brian Van der Horst, *Valerie Solanas Interview*, in *Scenes* (col.), in *The Village Voice* (New York, N.Y.), vol. XXII, no. 30, Jul. 25, 1977, p. 32, col. 2.

[40] Violet, Ultra. *Famous For 15 Minutes: My Years With Andy Warhol*. N.Y.: Avon Books (1st Avon Books Trade Printing Apr. 1990, © 1988) (ISBN 0-380-70843-4), p. v (Disclaimer) (esp. "I have taken artistic license in conveying both reality and essence" & "[s]ome conversations ... are not intended ... as verbatim quotes.").

[41] *Famous For 15 Minutes, op. cit.*, pp. 183–189. (Ultra objects, at p. 189, to assassination; for a possible contrast in her views, see *id.*, p. 241, for another near-killing of Andy Warhol.)

[42] Watson, Steven (2003). *Factory Made: Warhol and the Sixties*. Pantheon Books. pp. 425. ISBN 0-679-42372-9.

[43] Harron, Mary, & Daniel Minahan, *I Shot Andy Warhol* (N.Y.: Grove Press, 1st ed. 1995 (introduction © 1996) (ISBN 0-8021-3491-2)), p. xxxi (context per pp. xxx–xxxi) (*Introduction: On Valerie Solanas* (N.Y.: May 1996), *id.*, pp. vii–xxxi).

[44] B. Ruby Rich. "I Shot Andy Warhol" (http://history.sundance.org/films/1347). *Archives*. Sundance Institute. . Retrieved 27 November 2011.

[45] Michael Schaub (November 2003). "The 'Idiot Madness' of Valerie Solanis" (http://www.bookslut.com/propaganda/2003_11_000965.php). Bookslut. . Retrieved 27 November 2011.

[46] Neil Genzlinger (2001). "Theater Review; A Writer One Day, a Would-Be Killer the Next: Reliving the Warhol Shooting" (http://www.nytimes.com/2001/03/01/theater/theater-review-writer-one-day-would-be-killer-next-reliving-warhol-shooting.html). *Andy Warhol*. New York Times. . Retrieved 27 November 2011.

[47] C. Carr (2003). "SCUM Goddess: Who's the Villain? Who's the Saint?" (http://www.villagevoice.com/content/printVersion/176715/). Village Voice. . Retrieved 27 November 2011.

[48] Peter Marks (2011). "Theater review: 'Pop!' paints bold portrait of Warhol and his inner circle" (http://www.washingtonpost.com/lifestyle/style/theater-review-pop-paints-bold-portrait-of-warhol-and-his-inner-circle/2011/07/19/gIQAjEgaOI_story.html). *Style*. Washington Post. . Retrieved 27 November 2011.

[49] "Sara Stridsberg wins the Literature Prize" (http://www.norden.org/en/news-and-events/news/sara-stridsberg-wins-the-literature-prize). *News*. Norden. 2007. . Retrieved 27 November 2011.

[50] Pauline Oliveros. "To Valerie Solanas and Marilyn Monroe in Recognition of Their Desperation (1970)" (http://www.deeplistening.org/site/content/valerie-solanas-and-marilyn-monroe-recognition-their-desperation-1970-0). Deep Listening. . Retrieved 27 November 2011.

[51] "Pauline Oliveros" (http://roaratorio.com/21.html). Roaratorio. . Retrieved 27 November 2011.

[52] "Café Dansant: The Valerie Solanas & The Hired Guns + dj Ivan Scheldeman" (http://vooruit.be/en/event/2166). *Concerts*. Vooruit. 2010. . Retrieved 27 November 2011.

[53] James Martin Harding (25 February 2010). *Cutting performances: collage events, feminist artists, and the American avant-garde* (http:// books.google.com/books?id=IX8kznQvH54C&pg=PA151). University of Michigan Press. pp. 151–173. ISBN 978-0-472-11718-5. . Retrieved 27 November 2011.

References

External links

- *About Valerie Solanas* (http://www.womynkind.org/valbio.htm), by Freddie Baer (1999)
- *Whose Soiree Now?* (http://www.villagevoice.com/theater/0108,solomon,22438,11.html), by Alisa Solomon (Village Voice, February 2001)
- *Valerie Jean Solanas (1936-88)* (http://books.guardian.co.uk/news/articles/0,,1432425,00.html) (Guardian Unlimited, March 2005)
- A clip from *I, a Man* (http://www.videosurf.com/video/i-a-man-part-7-71664436), with Solanas and Tom Baker.
- Valerie Solanas bibliography (http://web.archive.org/web/20050817015943/http://geocities.com/ WestHollywood/Village/6982/solanas.html)
- Valerie Solanas (http://www.findagrave.com/cgi-bin/fg.cgi?page=gr&GRid=14927731) at *Find a Grave*
- *NNDB reference with picture* (http://www.nndb.com/people/212/000025137/): NNDB
- *"The Shot That Shattered the Velvet Underground"* (http://blogs.villagevoice.com/runninscared/2010/05/ andy_warhol_sho.php), *written June 6, 1968, from the Village Voice archives.*

Gloria Steinem

Gloria Steinem	
Gloria Steinem at a news conference, Women's Action Alliance, January 12, 1972	
Born	March 25, 1934 Toledo, Ohio, USA
Alma mater	Smith College[1]
Occupation	Writer and journalist for *Ms.* magazine and *New York* magazine
Political movement	Feminism
Spouse	David Bale (2000–2003, until his death)

Gloria Marie Steinem (born March 25, 1934) is an American feminist, journalist, and social and political activist who became nationally recognized as a leader of, and media spokeswoman for, the women's liberation movement in the late 1960s and 1970s. A prominent writer and political figure, Steinem has founded many organizations and projects and has been the recipient of many awards and honors. She was a columnist for *New York* magazine and co-founded *Ms.* magazine. In 1969, she published an article, *"After Black Power, Women's Liberation"* which, along with her early support of abortion rights, catapulted her to national fame as a feminist leader. In 2005, Steinem worked alongside Jane Fonda and Robin Morgan to co-found the Women's Media Center, an organization that works to amplify the voices of women in the media through advocacy, media and leadership training, and the creation of original content. Steinem currently serves on the board of the organization. She continues to involve herself in politics and media affairs as a commentator, writer, lecturer, and organizer, campaigning for candidates and reforms and publishing books and articles.

Early life

Steinem was born in Toledo, Ohio. Her mother, Ruth (née Nuneviller), was a Presbyterian of Scottish and German descent, and her father, Leo Steinem, was the son of Jewish immigrants from Germany and Poland.[2][3] The Steinems lived and traveled about in the trailer from which Leo carried out his trade as a traveling antiques dealer.[4]

When Steinem was only a few years old, her mother Ruth, then aged 34, had a "nervous breakdown" that left her an invalid, trapped in delusional fantasies that occasionally turned violent. She changed "from an energetic, fun-loving, book-loving" woman into "someone who was afraid to be alone, who could not hang on to reality long enough to hold a job, and who could rarely concentrate enough to read a book."[5] Ruth spent long periods in and out of sanatoriums for the mentally disabled. Steinem was only ten years old when her parents finally separated in 1944. Her father went to California to find work, while she and her mother continued to live together in Toledo.

While her parents divorced as a result of her mother's illness, it was not a result of chauvinism on the father's part, and Steinem claims to have "understood and never blamed him for the breakup."[6] Nevertheless, the impact of these events had a formative effect on her personality: while her father, a traveling salesman, had never provided much financial stability to the family, his exit aggravated their situation. Steinem interpreted her mother's inability to hold on to a job as evidence of general hostility towards working women.[7] She also interpreted the general apathy of doctors towards her mother as emerging from a similar anti-woman animus.[7] Years later, Steinem described her mother's experiences as having been pivotal to her understanding of social injustices. These perspectives convinced Steinem that women lacked social and political equality.[8]:129-138

Steinem attended Waite High School in Toledo and Western High School in Washington, D.C., from where she graduated. She then attended Smith College,[1] an institution with which she continues to remain engaged. In the late 1950s, Steinem spent two years in India as a Chester Bowles Asian Fellow.[9] After returning to the U.S., she served as director of the secretly CIA-funded Independent Research Service, and worked to send non-communist American students to the 1959 World Youth Festival.[10] In 1960, she was hired by Warren Publishing as the first employee of *Help!* magazine.[11]

Journalism career

Esquire magazine features editor Clay Felker gave freelance writer Steinem what she later called her first "serious assignment," regarding contraception; he didn't like her first draft and had her re-write the article.[12] Her resulting 1962 article[12] about the way in which women are forced to choose between a career and marriage preceded Betty Friedan's book *The Feminine Mystique* by one year.

In 1963, working on an article for Huntington Hartford's *Show* magazine, Steinem was employed as a Playboy Bunny at the New York Playboy Club.[13] The article featured a photo of Steinem in Bunny uniform and detailed how women were treated at those clubs. Steinem's experience as a Playboy Bunny was later made into the 1985 movie *A Bunny's Tale*. For a brief period after the article was published, Steinem was unable to land other assignments, but that situation did not last long;[14] indeed, Steinem landed a job at Felker's newly founded *New York* magazine in 1968.[12] In 1972, she co-founded the feminist-themed *Ms.* magazine. It began as a special edition of *New York*, and Felker funded the first issue.[12] When the first regular issue hit the news stands in July 1972, its 300,000 "one-shot" test copies sold out nationwide in three days. She even labeled it Spring Issue 1972 for that sole reason. It generated an astonishing 26,000 subscription orders and over 20,000 reader letters within weeks. Steinem would continue to write for the magazine until it was sold in 1987. The magazine changed hands again in 2001, to the Feminist Majority Foundation; Steinem remains on the masthead as one of six founding editors and serves on the advisory board.[15]

Political awakening and activism

Steinem actively campaigned for the Equal Rights Amendment, in addition to other laws and social reforms that promoted equality between women and men, helping to strike down many long-standing sex discriminatory laws, such as those that gave men superior rights in marriage and denied women equal economic opportunities. She also founded and co-founded many groups, including the Women's Action Alliance, on which she served as chair of the board throughout the 1970s, the NWPC, the Coalition of Labor Union Women, the Ms. Foundation for Women, Choice USA, and Women's Media Center.

In 1968, she signed the "Writers and Editors War Tax Protest" pledge, vowing to refuse tax payments in protest against the Vietnam War.[16]

After conducting a series of celebrity interviews, Steinem eventually got a political assignment covering George McGovern's presidential campaign. In 1969, she published an article, *"After Black Power, Women's Liberation"*[17] which, along with her early support of abortion rights, catapulted her to national fame as a feminist leader. Steinem brought other notable feminists to the fore and toured the country with lawyer Florynce Rae "Flo" Kennedy. In 1970 Gloria Steinem established herself as a leader of the Women's Movement with her impassioned Senate testimony in favor of the Equal Rights Amendment and her essay on a utopia of equality, *"What It Would Be Like If Women Win"*, in *Time* magazine. While Steinem would clash with both the older generation of women's rights leaders, most prominently Betty Friedan, as well as the younger, more militant Women's Liberation activists, she would gain a large, diverse, and multi-partisan following and become, alongside Friedan, the Women's Rights Movement's most prominent and influential spokesperson and leader. In 1970 she led the New York City march of the nation-wide Women's Strike for Equality alongside Friedan and then-Congressional candidate Bella Abzug. As the postergirl of the Feminist Movement, Steinem frequently appeared on news shows, television talk shows and specials, and on the covers of newspapers and magazines such as *Newsweek, Time, McCall's, People, New Woman, Ms.*, and *Parade*.

On July 10, 1971, Steinem, along with other feminist leaders (including Betty Friedan, Fannie Lou Hamer, Myrlie Evers, and several U.S. Representatives, including Shirley Chisholm and Bella Abzug) founded the National Women's Political Caucus (NWPC). An influential co-convener of the Caucus, she delivered her memorable "Address to the Women of America":

> This is no simple reform. It really is a revolution. Sex and race because they are easy and visible differences have been the primary ways of organizing human beings into superior and inferior groups and into the cheap labor on which this system still depends. We are talking about a society in which there will be no roles other

than those chosen or those earned. We are really talking about humanism.[18]

The next year Steinem became the founding editor and publisher of *Ms.* magazine, which speedily became a success, bringing feminist issues to the forefront of society and the media, quickly becoming the movement's most influential publication. In 1972, she also played a prominent role at the Democratic National Convention where she supported Shirley Chisholm's candidacy. That year Steinem and the NWPC had successfully organized bipartisan efforts to increase the representation of women at both major party conventions. In the early 1970s Steinem became the first woman to address the National Press Club.

In May 1975, Redstockings, a radical feminist group, raised the question of whether Steinem had continuing ties with the Central Intelligence Agency (CIA).[19][20] Though she admitted to having worked for a CIA-financed foundation in the late 1950s and early 1960s, Steinem denied any continuing involvement.[21] Steinem was also a member of Democratic Socialists of America.[22] In 1984 Steinem was arrested along with a number of members of Congress and civil rights activists for disorderly conduct outside the South African embassy while protesting against the South African apartheid system.[23]

Steinem co-founded the Coalition of Labor Union Women in 1974, and participated in the National Conference of Women in Houston, Texas in 1977. She became *Ms.* magazine's consulting editor when it was revived in 1991, and she was inducted into the National Women's Hall of Fame in 1993.[24]

Steinem played a variety of roles within the Women's Action Alliance, whose initial mission was "to stimulate and assist women at the local level to organize around specific action projects aimed at eliminating concrete manifestations of economic and social discrimination.".[25] She chaired the board from 1971-1978.

Steinem was active in working for civil rights for African Americans, Hispanics, and other minorities, working alongside civil rights leaders like Coretta Scott King and César Chávez, and took a public stance in opposition to the Vietnam War and in favor of gay rights.

In later years, Steinem became an outspoken supporter of animal rights, writing letters to the National Institutes of Health Office of Research on Women's Health urging the office director to end the "cruelty, fraud, and waste" of NIH-funded experiments on animals purportedly conducted in the name of advancing women's health.[26] She also became involved in international women's issues such as the campaign against female genital mutilation in Eastern countries and human trafficking.

Contrary to popular belief, Steinem did not coin the feminist slogan "A woman needs a man like a fish needs a bicycle." The phrase is actually attributable to Irina Dunn.[27] Indeed, she once dated publisher and real-estate developer Mortimer Zuckerman. [28]

Later life

In the 1980s and 1990s, Steinem had to deal with a number of personal setbacks, including the diagnosis of breast cancer in 1986[29] and trigeminal neuralgia in 1994.[30]

In 1992, Steinem co-founded Choice USA, a non-profit organization that mobilizes and provides ongoing support to a younger generation that lobbies for reproductive choice.[31] Her book *Revolution from Within: A Book of Self-Esteem* published that year was criticized for misrepresenting statistics regarding the incidence and lethality of anorexia nervosa. [32][33]

At the outset of the Gulf War, Steinem, along with prominent feminists Robin Morgan and Kate Millett, publicly opposed an incursion into the Middle East and asserted that ostensible goal of "defending democracy" was a pretense.[34]

During the Clarence Thomas sexual harassment scandal, Steinem voiced strong support for Anita Hill and suggested that one day Hill herself would sit on the Supreme Court.[35] According to two *Frontline* features (aired in 1995) and *Ms.* magazine, Steinem became an advocate for children she believed had been sexually abused by caretakers in day care centers (such as the McMartin preschool case).[36][37] In a 1998 press interview, Steinem weighed in on the Clinton impeachment hearings when asked whether President Bill Clinton should be impeached for lying under oath, she was quoted as saying, "Clinton should be censured for lying under oath about Lewinsky in the Paula Jones deposition, perhaps also for stupidity in answering at all."[38] The same year, Steinem defended Clinton against allegations of sexual impropriety that had been made by White House volunteer Kathleen Willey.[39]

On September 3, 2000, at age 66, Steinem married David Bale,[1] father of actor Christian Bale. The wedding was performed at the home of her friend Wilma Mankiller, the first female Principal Chief of the Cherokee Nation.[40] Steinem and Bale were married for only three years before he died of brain lymphoma on December 30, 2003, at age 62.[41]

Involvement in political campaigns

Steinem has been an influential figure in politics since the 1960s. Her involvement in presidential campaigns stretches back to her support of Adlai Stevenson in the 1952 presidential campaign.[42]

1968 election

A proponent of civil rights and fierce critic of the Vietnam War, Steinem was initially drawn to Senator Eugene McCarthy because of his "admirable record" on those issues. But in meeting and hearing him speak, she found him "cautious, uninspired, and dry."[8]:87 Interviewing him for *New York Magazine*, she called his answers a "fiasco," noting that he gave "not one spontaneous reply." As the campaign progressed, Steinem became baffled at "personally vicious" attacks that McCarthy leveled against his primary opponent Robert Kennedy, even as "his real opponent, Hubert Humphrey, went free."[8]:88

On a late-night radio show, Steinem garnered attention for declaring, "George McGovern is the real Eugene McCarthy."[43] Steinem had met McGovern in 1963 on the way to an economic conference organized by John Kenneth Galbraith and had been impressed by his unpretentious manner and genuine consideration of her opinions. Five years later in 1968, Steinem was chosen to pitch the arguments to McGovern as to why he should enter the presidential race that year. He agreed, and Steinem "consecutively or simultaneously served as pamphlet writer, advance "man", fund raiser, lobbyist of delegates, errand runner, and press secretary."[8]:95

McGovern lost the nomination in the infamous 1968 Democratic National Convention in Chicago. Steinem gave McGovern credit for standing on the platform with Humphrey in a show of unity after Humphrey had clinched the nomination, whereas McCarthy refused the same gesture. She later wrote of her astonishment at Humphrey's "refusal even to suggest to Chicago Mayor Richard J. Daley that he control the rampaging police and the bloodshed in the streets."[8]:96

1972 election

By the 1972 election, the Women's Movement was rapidly expanding its political power. Steinem, along with National Organization for Women founder Betty Friedan, Congresswomen Shirley Chisholm and Bella Abzug, and others, had founded the National Women's Political Caucus in July 1971.[44] Steinem attempted to run as a national delegate in support of Chisholm's presidential campaign.[45]

Nevertheless, Steinem was reluctant to re-join the McGovern campaign. Though she had brought in McGovern's single largest campaign contributor in 1968, she "*still* had been treated like a frivolous pariah by much of McGovern's campaign staff." In April 1972, Steinem remarked that he "still doesn't understand the Women's Movement."[8]:114

McGovern ultimately excised the abortion issue from the party's platform. (Recent publications show McGovern was deeply conflicted on the issue.[46]) Actress and activist Shirley MacLaine, though privately supporting abortion rights, urged the delegates to vote against the plank. Steinem later wrote this description of the events:

> The consensus of the meeting of women delegates held by the caucus had been to fight for the minority plank on reproductive freedom; indeed our vote had supported the plank nine to one. So fight we did, with three women delegates speaking eloquently in its favor as a constitutional right. One male Right-to-Life zealot spoke against, and Shirley MacLaine also was an opposition speaker, on the grounds that this *was* a fundamental right but didn't belong in the platform. We made a good showing. Clearly we would have won if McGovern's forces had left their delegates uninstructed and thus able to vote their consciences.[8]:100-110

Germaine Greer flatly contradicted Steinem's account. Having recently gained public notoriety for her feminist manifesto *The Female Eunuch* and sparring with Norman Mailer, Greer was commissioned to cover the convention for *Harper's Magazine*. Greer criticized Steinem's "controlled jubilation" that 38% of the delegates were women, ignoring the fact that "many delegations had merely stacked themselves with token females... The McGovern machine had already pulled the rug out from under them."[47]

Greer leveled her most searing critique on Steinem for her capitulation on abortion rights. Greer reported, "Jacqui Ceballos called from the crowd to demand abortion rights on the Democratic platform, but Bella [Abzug] and Gloria stared glassily out into the room," thus killing the abortion rights platform. Greer asks, "Why had Bella and Gloria not helped Jacqui to nail him on abortion? What reticence, what loserism had afflicted them?"[47] Steinem later recalled that the 1972 Convention was the only time Greer and Steinem ever met.[48]

The cover of Harper's that month read, "Womanlike, they did not want to get tough with their man, and so, womanlike, they got screwed."[49]

2004 election

In the run-up to the 2004 election, Steinem voiced fierce criticism of the Bush administration, asserting, "There has never been an administration that has been more hostile to women's equality, to reproductive freedom as a fundamental human right, and has acted on that hostility." She went on to claim, "If he is elected in 2004, abortion will be criminalized in this country."[50] At a Planned Parenthood event in Boston, Steinem declared Bush "a danger to health and safety," citing his antagonism to the Clean Water Act, reproductive freedom, sex education, and AIDS relief.[51]

2008 election

Steinem was an active participant in the 2008 presidential campaign. She praised both the Democratic front-runners, commenting,

> Both Senators Clinton and Obama are civil rights advocates, feminists, environmentalists, and critics of the war in Iraq.... Both have resisted pandering to the right, something that sets them apart from any Republican candidate, including John McCain. Both have Washington and foreign policy experience; George W. Bush did not when he first ran for president.[52]

Nevertheless, Steinem endorsed Senator Clinton, citing her broader experience, saying that the nation was in such bad shape it may require two terms of Clinton and two of Obama to fix it.[53]

She made headlines for a *New York Times* op-ed in which she cited gender and not race "probably the most restricting force in American life". She elaborated, "Black men were given the vote a half-century before women of any race were allowed to mark a ballot, and generally have ascended to positions of power, from the military to the boardroom, before any women."[54] This was attacked, however, from critics saying that white women were given the vote unabridged in 1920, whereas many blacks, female or male, could not vote until the Voting Rights Act of 1965, and some were lynched for trying, and that many white women advanced in the business and political worlds before black women and men.[55]

Steinem in November 2008

Steinem again drew attention for, according to the *New York Observer*, seeming "to denigrate the importance of John McCain's time as a prisoner of war in Vietnam". Steinem's broader argument "was that the media and the political world are too admiring of militarism in all its guises."[56]

Steinem was vocal in criticising the media treatment of the Clinton campaign as sexist. Following McCain's selection of Sarah Palin as his running mate, Steinem penned an op-ed in which she labeled Palin an "unqualified woman" who "opposes everything most other women want and need." Steinem described her nomination speech as "divisive and deceptive", called for a more inclusive Republican Party and concluded that Palin resembled "Phyllis Schlafly, only younger."[57]

Feminist positions

Steinem's social and political views overlap into multiple schools of feminism. This problem is compounded by the evolution of her views over five decades of activism. Although most frequently considered a liberal feminist, Steinem has repeatedly characterized herself as a radical feminist.[58] More importantly, she has repudiated categorization within feminism as "nonconstructive to specific problems. "I've turned up in every category. So it makes it harder for me to take the divisions with great seriousness."[59] Nevertheless, on concrete issues, Steinem has staked firm positions.

Abortion

Steinem is a staunch advocate of *reproductive freedom*, a term she herself coined and helped popularize. She credits the *Webster v. Reproductive Health Services* hearings she covered[60][61] for *New York Magazine* as the event that turned her into an activist.[62] At the time, abortions were widely illegal and risky. In 2005, Steinem appeared in the documentary film *I Had an Abortion* by Jennifer Baumgardner and Gillian Aldrich. In the film, Steinem described the abortion she had as a young woman in London, where she lived briefly before studying in India. In the documentary *My Feminism*, Steinem characterized her abortion as a "pivotal and constructive experience."

Pornography

Along with Susan Brownmiller and Catharine MacKinnon, Steinem has been a vehement critic of pornography, which she distinguishes from erotica: "Erotica is as different from pornography as love is from rape, as dignity is from humiliation, as partnership is from slavery, as pleasure is from pain." Steinem's argument hinges on the distinction between reciprocity versus domination. She writes, "Blatant or subtle, pornography involves no equal power or mutuality. In fact, much of the tension and drama comes from the clear idea that one person is dominating the other." On the issue of same-sex pornography, Steinem asserts, "Whatever the gender of the participants, all pornography is an imitation of the male-female, conqueror-victim paradigm, and almost all of it actually portrays or implies enslaved women and master." Steinem also cites "snuff films" as a serious threat to women.[8]:219[63]

Genital mutilation

Steinem wrote the definitive article on female genital mutilation that brought the practice into the American public's consciousness.[8]:292[64] The article reports on the "75 million women suffering with the results of genital mutilation." According to Steinem, "The real reasons for genital mutilation can only be understood in the context of the patriarchy: men must control women's bodies as the means of production, and thus repress the independent power of women's sexuality." Steinem's article contains the basic arguments that would be developed by philosopher Martha Nussbaum.[65]

On male circumcision, she commented, "These patriarchal controls limit men's sexuality too... That's why men are asked symbolically to submit the sexual part of themselves and their sons to patriarchal authority, which seems to be the origin of male circumcision, a practice that, even as advocates admit, is medically unnecessary 90% of the time. Speaking for myself, I stand with many brothers in eliminating that practice too."[66]

Same-sex marriage

Steinem has expressed support for same-sex marriage, stating "The idea that sexuality is only okay if it ends in reproduction oppresses women—whose health depends on separating sexuality from reproduction—as well as gay men and lesbians."[67] Steinem is also a signatory of the manifesto, "Beyond Same-Sex Marriage: A New Strategic Vision For All Our Families and Relationships", which advocates for extending legal rights and privileges to a wide range of relationships, households, and families.[68]

Transsexualism

Steinem has questioned transsexualism. In 1977, she expressed disapproval that the heavily publicized sex-role change of tennis player Renée Richards had been characterized as "a frightening instance of what feminism could lead to" or as "living proof that feminism isn't necessary." Steinem wrote, "At a minimum, it was a diversion from the widespread problems of sexual inequality." She writes that, while she supports the right of individuals to identify as they choose, she claims that, in many cases, transsexuals "surgically mutilate their own bodies" in order to conform to a gender role that is inexorably tied to physical body parts. She concludes that "feminists are right to feel uncomfortable about the need for and uses of transsexualism." The article concluded with what became one of Steinem's most famous quotes: "If the shoe doesn't fit, must we change the foot?" Although clearly meant in the context of transsexuality, the quote is frequently mistaken as a general statement about feminism.[8]:206-210

Prominent feminists including Judith Butler, Eve Sedgwick, and Donna Haraway have rejected Steinem's argument, embracing ideas of "queerness" and "the abject other" as vital to the destabilization and subversion of normative constraints.[69] :223-441 In August 2008, Steinem responded to claims that she "condemned transsexualism", saying that is something she "absolutely had never done."[70]

Feminist theory

Steinem has repeatedly voiced her disapproval of the obscurantism and abstractions prevalent in feminist academic theorizing. She said, "Nobody cares about feminist academic writing. That's careerism. These poor women in academia have to talk this silly language that nobody can understand in order to be accepted...But I recognize the fact that we have this ridiculous system of tenure, that the whole thrust of academia is one that values education, in my opinion, in inverse ratio to its usefulness—and what you write in inverse relationship to its understandability."[71] Steinem later singled out deconstructionists like Judith Butler for criticism: "I always wanted to put a sign up on the road to Yale saying, 'Beware: Deconstruction Ahead'. Academics are forced to write in language no one can understand so that they get tenure. They have to say 'discourse', not 'talk'. Knowledge that is not accessible is not helpful. It becomes aerialised."[72]

List of works

- *The Thousand Indias* (1957)
- *The Beach Book* (1963)
- *Outrageous Acts and Everyday Rebellions* (1983)
- *Marilyn: Norma Jean* (1986)
- *Revolution from Within* (1992)
- *Moving beyond Words* (1993)
- *Doing Sixty & Seventy* (2006)

Biographies

- *The Education of A Woman: The Life and Times of Gloria Steinem* by Carolyn Heilbrun (1995)
- *Gloria Steinem: Her Passions, Politics, and Mystique* by Sydney Ladenshon Stern (1997)

Documentaries about Gloria Steinem

Gloria: In Her Own Words, a documentary first aired on HBO in 2011 [73]

References

[1] "Gloria Steinem" (http://www.biography.com/articles/Gloria-Steinem-9493491). Biography.com. . Retrieved June 1, 2010.
[2] Gloria Steinem (http://jwa.org/feminism/_html/JWA067.htm), *Jewish Women's Archive*. Retrieved 2010-06-01
[3] Ancestry of Gloria Steinem (http://www.wargs.com/other/steinem.html)
[4] http://jwa.org/encyclopedia/article/steinem-gloria
[5] Steinem, Gloria (1983). *Outrageous Acts and Everyday Rebellions*.
[6] Marcello, Patricia. Gloria Steinem: A Biography. Westport, CT: Greenwood Press, 2004. p. 20.
[7] Marcello, Patricia. Gloria Steinem: A Biography. Westport, CT: Greenwood Press, 2004.
[8] Steinem, Gloria (1984). *Outrageous Acts and Everyday Rebellions* (1 ed.). New York: Henry Holt & Co..
[9] Bird, Kai (1992). *The Chairman: John J. McCloy, the making of the American establishment*. Simon & Schuster. pp. 483–484.
[10] "C.I.A. Subsidized Festival Trips; Hundreds of Students Were Sent to World Gatherings" (http://select.nytimes.com/gst/abstract. html?res=F20C1FFD3B5F137A93C3AB1789D85F438685F9&scp=2&sq=Gloria+Steinem+CIA&st=p). *The New York Times*. February 21, 1967. .
[11] Cooke, Jon. "Wrightson's Warren Days" (http://twomorrows.com/comicbookartist/articles/04warren.html). TwoMorrows. . Retrieved June 1, 2010.
[12] Mclellan, Dennis (July 2, 2008). "Clay Felker, 82; editor of New York magazine led New Journalism charge" (http://articles.latimes.com/ 2008/jul/02/local/me-felker2). *Los Angeles Times*. . Retrieved 2008-11-23.
[13] Kolhatkar, Sheelah (December 18, 2005). "Gloria Steinem" (http://www.observer.com/node/38125). The New York Observer. . Retrieved June 1, 2010.
[14] Minnesota Public Radio interview, June 15, at 32:40 (http://minnesota.publicradio.org/display/web/2009/06/15/midmorning1/)
[15] *Ms. Magazine History* (http://www.msmagazine.com/about.asp)
[16] "Writers and Editors War Tax Protest" January 30, 1968 *New York Post*
[17] Steinem, Gloria (April 4, 1969). "After Black Power, Women's Liberation" (http://nymag.com/news/politics/46802/). New York. . Retrieved June 01, 2010.
[18] Johnson Lewis, Jone. "Gloria Steinem Quotes" (http://womenshistory.about.com/cs/quotes/a/qu_g_steinem.htm). About. .
[19] "Gloria Steinem and the CIA" NameBase.Org Report (http://www.namebase.org/steinem.html)
[20] Document obtained through Freedom of Information Act and published by Redstockings, re. Steinem reporting on Vienna Youth Festival activists. Redstockings' 1975 Report (http://www.namebase.org/foia/festival.html)

[21] Harrington, Stephanie (July 4, 1976). "It Changed My Life" (http://www.nytimes.com/1976/07/04/books/friedan-changed.html/). *The New York Times*.

[22] "Our Structure" (http://www.dsausa.org/about/structure.html). Democratic Socialists of America. .

[23] "Arrested at embassy" (http://news.google.com/newspapers?id=97YfAAAAIBAJ&pg=2393,5208721). *Gadsden Times*: p. A10. 20 December 1984. .

[24] *Women's of the Hall*. (http://greatwomen.org/women.php?action=viewone&id=150)

[25] http://asteria.fivecolleges.edu/findaids/sophiasmith/mnsss76_bioghist.html

[26] Steinem to NIH: Stop 'Triple Injustice' of 'Cruelty, Fraud, and Waste'!. (http://www.femfatalities.com/feat-steinem.asp"Gloria)

[27] "A woman needs a man like a fish needs a bicycle" (http://www.phrases.org.uk/meanings/414150.html). The Phrase Finder. .

[28] http://wrmea.org/component/content/article/253/4734-mortimer-zuckerman-two-voices-but-both-talking-about-himself.html

[29] Holt, Patricia (September 22, 1995). "Making Ms.Story / The biography of Gloria Steinem, a woman of controversy and contradictions" (http://www.sfgate.com/cgi-bin/article.cgi?file=/chronicle/archive/1995/09/24/RV65259.DTL). *The San Francisco Chronicle*. .

[30] Mother Jones. *Gloria* (http://www.motherjones.com/news/qa/1995/11/gorney.html)

[31] Choice USA (http://www.choiceusa.org/index.php?option=com_content&task=view&id=77&Itemid=2)

[32] Sheaffer, Robert (April 1997). "Feminism, the Noble Lie" (http://www.debunker.com/texts/noblelie.html). Free Inquiry Magazine. .

[33] Grenier, Richard (July 25, 1994). "Feminists falsify facts for effect – controversy over Gloria Steinem's use of anorexia death statistics stirs controversy over exaggeration for political effect" (http://findarticles.com/p/articles/mi_m1571/is_n30_v10/ai_15640024/). Insight on the News. .

[34] Steinem, Gloria (January 20, 1991). "We Learned the Wrong Lessons in Vietnam; A Feminist Issue Still" (http://www.nytimes.com/1991/01/20/opinion/l-we-learned-the-wrong-lessons-in-vietnam-a-feminist-issue-still-839991.html). New York Times. .

[35] Sontag, Deborah (April 26, 1992). "Anita Hill and Revitalizing Feminism" (http://www.nytimes.com/1992/04/26/nyregion/anita-hill-and-revitalizing-feminism.html). The New York Times. .

[36] "The Search for Satan" (http://www.pbs.org/wgbh/pages/frontline/flfeedback/readflfeedbacksatan.html). PBS Frontline. 1995. .

[37] Irvine, Martha (October 8, 1999). "Psychiatrist Has License Suspended" (http://www.rickross.com/reference/satanism/satanism61.html). The Associated Press. .

[38] "Steinem Wants Clinton Censured, Not Impeached" (http://www.feminist.org/news/newsbyte/uswirestory.asp?id=852). Reuters: September 28, 1998. . Retrieved 2007-06-08.

[39] Young, Cathy (September 1998). "Groping towards sanity" (http://www.reason.com/news/show/30734.html). Reason. .

[40] "Feminist icon Gloria Steinem first-time bride at 66" (http://web.archive.org/web/20070917071020/http://archives.cnn.com/2000/US/09/05/steinem.marriage.ap/index.html). CNN.com. September 5, 2000. Archived from the original (http://archives.cnn.com/2000/US/09/05/steinem.marriage.ap/index.html) on 2007-09-17. .

[41] von Zeilbauer, Paul (January 1, 2004). "David Bale, 62, Activist and Businessman" (http://www.nytimes.com/2004/01/01/us/david-bale-62-activist-and-businessman.html). The New York Times. .

[42] Lazo, Caroine. *Gloria Steinem: Feminist Extraordinaire*. New York: Lerner Publications, 1998. pp. 28.

[43] Miroff, Bruce. *The Liberals' Moment: The McGovern Insurgency and the Identity Crisis of the Democratic Party*. University Press of Kansas, 2007. pp. 206

[44] Miroff. pp. 205.

[45] Freeman, Jo (February 2005). "Shirley Chisholm's 1972 Presidential Campaign" (http://www.uic.edu/orgs/cwluherstory/jofreeman/polhistory/chisholm.htm). *University of Illinois at Chicago Women's History Project*. .

[46] Miroff. pp. 207.

[47] Harper's Magazine October 1972.

[48] Wow, April 16, 2009. "Gloria Steinem: Still Committing 'Outrageous Acts' at 75" (http://www.wowowow.com/politics/gloria-steinem-75-feminists-pro-choice-268505?page=0,3)

[49] Harper's Magazine Archives (http://harpers.org/archive/1972)

[50] Buzzflash Interview (http://www.buzzflash.com/interviews/04/02/int04008.html)

[51] Feminist Pioneer Gloria Steinem: "Bush is a Danger to Our Health and Safety" (http://www.democracynow.org/2004/7/26/feminist_pioneer_gloria_steinem_bush_is)

[52] Steinem, Gloria (February 7, 2007). "Right Candidates, Wrong Question" (http://www.nytimes.com/2007/02/07/opinion/07steinem.html?_r=1&oref=slogin). New York Times. . Retrieved 2009-07-01.

[53] Feldman, Claudia (September 18, 2007). "Has Gloria Steinem mellowed? No way" (http://www.chron.com/disp/story.mpl/life/5142732.html). The Houston Chronicle. .

[54] Steinem, Gloria. New York Times: *Women are Never the Front-runners* (http://www.nytimes.com/2008/01/08/opinion/08steinem.html?_r=1/)

[55] Gharib, Ali (January 16, 2008). "Democratic Race Sheds Issues for Identities" (http://www.ipsnews.net/news.asp?idnews=40811). Inter Press News. . Retrieved March 16, 2011.

[56] The New York Observer. *Stumping for Clinton, Steinem Says McCain's POW Cred Is Overrated* (http://www.observer.com/2008/stumping-clinton-steinem-says-mccains-p-o-w-cred-overrated/)

[57] "Palin: wrong woman, wrong message" (http://www.latimes.com/news/printedition/opinion/la-oe-steinem4-2008sep04,0,1290251.story)

[58] Marianne Schnall Interview (http://www.feminist.com/resources/artspeech/interviews/gloria.htm/)

[59] Interviewed By Cynthia Gorney: *Mother Jones* (http://www.motherjones.com/news/qa/1995/11/gorney.html/)

[60] Steinem, Gloria (July 1989), *A Basic Human Right*, **18**, Ms. Magazine, pp. 38–41, ISSN 00478318

[61] Copelon, Rhonda; Kolbert, Kathryn (July 1989), *Imperfect Justice*, **18**, Ms. Magazine, pp. 42–44, ISSN 00478318

[62] Benjamin, Scott (January 22, 2006). "No Slowdown For Gloria Steinem" (http://www.cbsnews.com/stories/2006/01/22/sunday/main1227391.shtml/). CBS News. .

[63] *Erotica and Pornography: A Clear and Present Difference*. Ms. Magazine. November 1978, pp. 53. & *Pornography--Not Sex but the Obscene Use of Power*. Ms. Magazine. August 1977, 43.

[64] "The International Crime of Female Genital Mutilation." *Ms. Magazine*, March 1979, pp. 65.

[65] Nussbaum, Martha C. *Sex & Social Justice*. New York: Oxford University Press, 1999. pp. 118-129.

[66] What have FGC opponents said publicly about male genital cutting? (http://www.noharmm.org/FGCsay.htm)

[67] Steptoe, Sonja; Steinem, Gloria (March 28, 2004). "10 Questions For Gloria Steinem" (http://www.time.com/time/magazine/article/0,9171,605468,00.html). Time Magazine. .

[68] "Signatories" (http://web.archive.org/web/20080420154202/www.beyondmarriage.org/signatories.html). *BeyondMarriage.org*. Archived from the original (http://www.beyondmarriage.org/signatories.html) on 2008-04-20. . Retrieved 2011-01-17.

[69] Butler, Judith (September 20, 1993). *Bodies That Matter: On the Discursive Limits of Sex*. Routledge. ISBN 978-0415903660.

[70] Gloria Steinem & Steve Scher (08-07-2008). *A Conversation with Gloria Steinem* (http://www.kuow.org/program.php?id=15524) (MP3). Seattle: KUOW. .

[71] Mother Jones. "Gloria Steinem" (http://www.motherjones.com/news/qa/1995/11/gorney.html/)

[72] Denes, Melissa (January 17, 2005). "'Feminism? It's hardly begun'" (http://www.guardian.co.uk/world/2005/jan/17/gender. melissadenes). London: The Guardian. .

[73] http://articles.latimes.com/2011/aug/15/entertainment/la-et-gloria-20110815

External links

- Official website (http://www.gloriasteinem.com)
- Profile (http://www.feminist.com/gloriasteinem/) at Feminist.com

Article Sources and Contributors

Radical feminism *Source*: http://en.wikipedia.org/w/index.php?oldid=456679117 *Contributors*: 159753, ALC, Academic Challenger, AdultSwim, Akradecki, AlexR, Alienus, Andrewpmk, Andycjp, AnnaAniston, Apocryphe, Arria Belli, Arthena, Askild, BKHal2007, Ben Standeven, Benw, Beste, Bierleka, Binksternet, Blackcats, Bluszczokrzew, BobV01, Bookandcoffee, Bparaguya, BryceHarrington, Caesarjbsquitti, Cailil, Caitcap, Candichurchill, Cantaire87, Carre, Catamorphism, Cerberus of elyssia, Cgingold, Chadbrochill13, Charl39, ChrisCork, Clairywarey, Cmichael, Conversion script, Cr0w bar, Cybermud, CyntWorkStuff, Dakinijones, Danger, Davewho2, Dbachmann, Dcoetzee, Deconstructhis, Defenestrate, Deville, Doviende, Dsmurat, Dwapollo, Dysprosia, ERcheck, Easter rising, Ebehn, El C, Elm-39, Emperor1993, Enlight, Erianna, Evie em, Eyu100, Falcon8765, Faunas, Fenice, Fifelfoo, Floaterfluss, Flyer22, Frankie816, Fratrep, FreplySpang, Fuzzform, Gaius Cornelius, GekkoGeck0, GhostPirate, Gilliam, GinaDana, Ginar, Graham87, Gtrmp, HJ Mitchell, Hallows AG, HarmonicFeather, Hertz1888, Hq3473, Hu12, Hyperjoy7, I Grave Rob, Iamcuriousblue, Invisible Noise, Iridescent, Irishguy, JCDenton2052, JHFTC, Jayunderscorezero, Jean-Jacques Georges, Jeff3000, Jmabel, JohnLauritsen, Jrtayloriv, JustAGal, KDCS, Kakofonous, Karen Johnson, Klbrengle, Kmweber, Koavf, Krellis, La Guiri, Lady Mondegreen, Landon1980, Laurenvo, LeilaA, Lights, Livajo, Loneranger4justice, Macboots, Matt620, Matthew Stannard, Melrose26, Mike.lifeguard, Misscorrect, Moink, Monty Cantsin, N1h11, Neitherday, Nick Levinson, Nicke Lilltroll, Nikai, Nikkicraft, Nixdorf, Nlu, Nosillochsoj, Ohlaurag, Omegatron, Onedayoneday, Owen, Panderous, Parthasarathy B, Paul Benjamin Austin, People Powered, Peter G Werner, Peter Karlsen, Pigman, Pinko1977, Radgeek, RatatoskJones, RememberingLife, Rich Farmbrough, Ringmaster j, Roastpotatoes, SU Linguist, Sardanaphalus, SchuminWeb, Sennasay, Shanoman, Shrike, Sketchesofskidrow, Sluzzelin, Snow Shoes, Speakwise, Spellcheck, Sseguin, Stephenb, Suprgye, TRFA, Taak, Taranet, Tedius Zanarukando, Tempodivalse, The Literate Engineer, Themfromspace, Tikiwont, Tomisti, Tony619, TonyW, Towsonu2003, Unleashthesoy, Unyoyega, Urod, Viriditas, VoluntarySlave, Woohookitty, Xxx Rock Tubs, YK Times, Zeus, 312 anonymous edits

Anarcha-feminism *Source*: http://en.wikipedia.org/w/index.php?oldid=463485536 *Contributors*: 4C, Adam Bishop, Aim Here, Anarcha, Andres, AndrewH, Anirvan, AnnaAniston, Apollonius 1236, Auntof6, AwOc, Belovedfreak, Blahblahblahblahblahblah, Cailil, Cantaire87, Carabinieri, Cast, Cbr2702, Cerberus of elyssia, Che y Marijuana, CommonsDelinker, Contributor777, Crltn, DNewhall, Dakinijones, Dan6hell66, Darkdaughta, Dawn Bard, Doviende, Eboda, Ebyabe, Eduen, Edward, Encephalon, Etcetc, Fang 23, Faré, Fifelfoo, Francs2000, Frank Shearar, Gaius Cornelius, Ginsengbomb, Gobonobo, Good Olfactory, Grrrlriot, Hagerman, Hajatvrc, HarisX, JCapone, JamesAM, Jonkerz, Jrtayloriv, Karimarie, Koavf, Kostisl, LMAOnade, Lectert, Lihaas, Livajo, Lquilter, Magister Mathematicae, MapsMan, Max rspct, Maziotis, Meco, MelmothX, Mesolimbo, Mikael V, Mikewazhere, Mladifilozof, Monty Cantsin, Mozric, Mr.Rocks, MrVoluntarist, N1h11, Nihilo 01, Obi777, Operation Spooner, Owen, Phil Sandifer, PhilLiberty, Pintorj2, Plrk, RJII, Revkat, Rich Farmbrough, Rjwilmsi, Roadcollective, Roarjo, Robert. Helms, Robgraham, SPresley, SarahStierch, Sardanaphalus, Saulisagenius, SimonP, Skomorokh, Smilo Don, Snow Shoes, Stefanomione, Stephenb, Stormydawn, Sunray, SusanLesch, The Ungovernable Force, Themfromspace, Thorpe, Timthepenguin, Tothebarricades.tk, Transform.everything, USchick, UnitedStatesian, Vis-a-visconti, Vision Thing, VoluntarySlave, W guice, Wadewitz, Woohookitty, Xe7al, Xomic, Zazaban, Δ, 92 anonymous edits

D. A. Clarke *Source*: http://en.wikipedia.org/w/index.php?oldid=449102825 *Contributors*: AnnaAniston, Bearcat, Cantaire87, Dev920, Discospinster, Dsp13, Geeksquad, Iamcuriousblue, John254, Kbdank71, Kingturtle, Kuyabribri, Peter G Werner, RecoveringTechnophile, Robofish, Scott MacDonald, The Literate Engineer, Tim1357, Treybien, Xavexgoem, 2 anonymous edits

Nikki Craft *Source*: http://en.wikipedia.org/w/index.php?oldid=460989914 *Contributors*: ***Ria777, Aaron Brenneman, Amire80, Anchoress, Atomaton, Bcorr, BodyPride, Bongwarrior, Coredesat, Dandelion1, Desertsky85451, Edwy, FloNight, Fourthords, Freakofnurture, Grendelkhan, Gurch, Herostratus, Iamcuriousblue, JayW, Jcuk, Johntex, Kingpin13, Larana, Leaveextra, Lionelt, Michaelbluejay, Murderbike, Musical Linguist, Nikkicraft, Nssdfdsfds, Nudistwriter, Only, Peter G Werner, Phil Boswell, Phuongj, Pigman, PinkCake, Quarl, Radgeek, Radicallove, Rich Farmbrough, RidinHood25, Rjwilmsi, SallyForth123, Samsara, Sdedeo, SimonLyall, Simonton, SmartGuy Old, Splash, Stephen B Streater, Stifle, StuffOfInterest, TheMidnighters, Threeafterthree, Thryduulf, Tom harrison, Tregoweth, Treybien, Tristessa de St Ange, Vegaswikian, Vlad, WAS 4.250, Wikipediatrix, Will Beback, 184 anonymous edits

Mujeres Creando *Source*: http://en.wikipedia.org/w/index.php?oldid=434791071 *Contributors*: Bearcat, Bolivian Unicyclist, Dybryd, Eduen, Emerson7, Good Olfactory, James086, Luceromarissa, N1h11, Neo139, Opiateofthemasses, Rich Farmbrough, Txomin, Uyvsdi, Vis-a-visconti, Wikignome0529, 6 anonymous edits

Mary Daly *Source*: http://en.wikipedia.org/w/index.php?oldid=459900263 *Contributors*: Adzze, Afterwriting, All Hallow's Wraith, Althaea, Amberjademwekali, Andycjp, Angusmclellan, Antandrus, Archanamiya, Avjoska, BCalum, BD2412, Bearcat, Bender235, Briancua, Brunohonurb, Canadian Paul, Captain panda, Ceyockey, D6, Danger, Danielfolsom, David.Throop, Dbachmann, Delirium, Demeter, Denisarona, Dev920, Dominus, Eastlaw, EhUpMother, El C, Elakhna, Emeraldcityserendipity, Emily100, Ephignia, Ephilei, EvaK, Everyking, Fieldday-sunday, Fisherjs, GeoGreg, HaereMai, Hinschelwood, Hyacinth, Incorrecto, Inwind, J.delanoy, JCDenton2052, JessicaSideways, Jhay116, JimVC3, Jjayson, Jleon, Johnpacklambert, Jrtayloriv, Jugbo, Kbdank71, Kelly Martin, Koavf, Ktr101, Libroman, Liv race, Lookatyougo, Makemi, Malik Shabazz, MangoWong, MarnetteD, Mattinbgn, Mensalina, Michaelbarreto, MsWonderland, Mwanner, NeoJustin, Ngies, Nick Levinson, Nicke Lilltroll, Nietzsche 2, Only, Owen, PDH, PatrickEricCampbell, Philip Cross, Philosophy Teacher, Poccil, Prezbo, Pv1888, Quadell, R'n'B, Rebelrsr, Redeagle688, Revaaron, Richard Arthur Norton (1958-), Rje, Rjwilmsi, Rms125a@hotmail.com, Robert Brockway, Robofish, Rudrasharman, SC Witch, Scythre, Shakehandsman, Shorne, Shunpiker, SimonP, Sonicyouth86, Spacini, Steve3742, Super Spy 0, TMiller11a, The Rambling Man, Tide rolls, Timo Honkasalo, Tinyrevolution, Towsonu2003, Transwarrior, Treybien, TutterMouse, Viriditas, WWGB, WhyDoIKeepForgetting, Wikifried, Wikkrockiana, WpFalcon, Xed, Your silence rots you, Zin, 145 anonymous edits

Andrea Dworkin *Source*: http://en.wikipedia.org/w/index.php?oldid=463422188 *Contributors*: ABCD, ACSE, Aaron Schulz, AaronSw, Active Banana, Adambiswanger1, Addere, Aim Here, Alansohn, Aldie, AllGloryToTheHypnotoad, Alpasel, Amorrow, AndreaCunkwin, Andres, Andrewlp1991, Andy Marchbanks, Anentiresleeve, Angr, AnkaraX, Anomalocaris, Anthony, Aristophanes68, Ashenai, AxelBoldt, BD2412, Baegis, Bearcat, Benw, Betacommand, Bickins Von Internet, Bill j, Bobblewik, Boomshadow, BradBeattie, BrainyBabe, Brian0918, Brighterorange, Brockert, Bullzeye, Bwithh, Calsicol, Cameron.walsh, Can't sleep, clown will eat me, Canglesea, CatherineMunro, Catherinebrown, Cerejota, Cohesion, Convit, CopperMurdoch, Coredesat, Creidieki, Crotalus horridus, Cryptico, Cueball, Curtsurly, CyntWorkStuff, DARTH SIDIOUS 2, DSatz, Daa89563, Dado, Danbarton, Daniel, Daniel C. Boyer, Daoi, Darklock, Darwinek, Davshul, Decltype, Diderot, Dismas, DocWatson42, Doczilla, Dogru144, Doovinator, Doviende, Dpol, Dreadstar, Dtobias, Dweller, Eclecticunderground, Eirelover@earthlink.net, El C, Eloquence, Elpincha, Elrith, Epbr123, Epsilon60198, Escape Orbit, Euchiasmus, Evercat, ExNoctem, Fabulous Creature, Flitzer, FloNight, Francine3, FreplySpang, Frozenevolution, Gaius Cornelius, Ggbroad, Gioueeoi, Grouf, Gscshoyru, Guttlekraw, Guy Harris, HOT L Baltimore, Hosadmin, Hu12, Iamcuriousblue, Iluvchineselit, Inter, Irk, IronDuke, JIP, JJstroker, JJstrokey, Jahsonic, Janejellyroll, Jayen466, Jezhotwells, Jmarob, Jojhutton, Jonathan.s.kt, Josh Parris, Joyous!, Jpgordon, JuJube, Jun Nijo, Just Jim Dandy, JustAGal, Jweiss11, KF, Kaiser187, Kalibhakta, Kasreyn, KatharineHepburn, Kbdank71, Kevinalewis, Knucmo2, Knulclunk, Koavf, Konczewski, Kootenayvolcano, Kunstlerpop, Laurelism, Leebo, Leisaie, Lightmouse, Ling.Nut, Lionelt, Lli12, Loren.wilton, Lugnuts, LukeL, MCTales, MShabazz, Malik Shabazz, Malinaccier, Mandarax, Mare Nostrum, Mbessey, Mccready, Mcsweet, Meanderthal, Meco, Meelar, Michael Devore, Michael Hardy, MinervaK, Mirv, MisfitToys, Moink, Montrealais, Moorlock, Moosnuff, Moshe Constantine Hassan Al-Silverburg, Motorizer, Mronimusha, Mspraveen, Mufka, NYCpresto, Natalie Erin, NawlinWiki, Nchase, Ndenison, Neutrality, Nick Levinson, Nietzsche 2, Nightscream, Nikkicraft, Nsigniacorp, O, Oatmeal batman, Obituarist, Oneiros, Opponent, Ortolan88, Oskar Sigvardsson, Owen, P Cezanne, Pacificus, Peter G Werner, Philip Trueman, Phiwum, Pinktulip, Ponyo, Prezbo, Pschelden, Questioning mkb, Qwertyus, R'n'B, R. fiend, Radgeek, Rich Farmbrough, RidinHood25, Rigby27, Ringbang, Rjwilmsi, Robert Bruce Livingston, Rohitde, Romarin, RyanGerbil10, SDC, SJP, SallyForth123, ScottFritz-DM, Sdedeo, Seaphoto, Seminumerical, Shadowjams, Shanes, Shmuel, Silly rabbit, SimonP, Simonton, Sj, Skomorokh, Slashme, SlimVirgin, Slref, Snoyes, Son of More, SpK, Standardfact, Steven Zhang, Sticky Parkin, Stockma, Stuarta, Swifteight, Tabercil, The Anome, The Literate Engineer, The Love Train, The Purple Nazz, The Thing That Should Not Be, TheCatalyst31, Theresa knott, Thymol1, Tide rolls, Timo Honkasalo, Tinton5, Tktktk, Tom harrison, Tony1, Touch Of Light, Tregoweth, Treybien, Tzahy, Utcursch, Vgranucci, Viajero, Vis-a-visconti, WLU, Wanglo, Wassermann, WhisperToMe, Woland1234, Wwmargera, Xed, Zoe, Zweifel, Алиса Селезньова, רופב"ני, 383 anonymous edits

Melissa Farley *Source*: http://en.wikipedia.org/w/index.php?oldid=462450611 *Contributors*: Aitias, Alan Liefting, Arthur Rubin, Auric, Axiomatica, Btwoodward, Cailil, Catamorphism, Catherinebrown, Chaz987654321, ContiAWB, CyntWorkStuff, David Gerard, Doczilla, EconProfessor, El C, Emc2, Enviroboy, Everyking, Foot Dragoon, Geodyde, Iamcuriousblue, IronAngelAlice, JamesAM, Jeepday, Jmlk17, John Carter, John Nevard, Joseph Solis in Australia, Jossi, Kleinzach, Lar, Lepiota, Lionelt, Mlaffs, Nikkicraft, Ninorc, OlympiaDiego, Onebravemonkey, Peter G Werner, Peter Karlsen, PhilKnight, Rich Farmbrough, Roomsmight, RyanRetroWickawack, SallyForth123, Sarah, Skapur, Spell4yr, Talorc, The Anome, Threeafterthree, Treybien, Updatehelper, Verbal, Vis-a-visconti, Vlad, Zodon, Шизомби, 60 anonymous edits

Sheila Jeffreys *Source*: http://en.wikipedia.org/w/index.php?oldid=435241955 *Contributors*: Asarelah, Ashley Y, AvicAWB, Booyabazooka, C.Fred, Calton, Chunky Rice, Closedmouth, Cuddy Wifter, D6, DarthVader, Eyedubya, Gabe boldt, Gnowor, GregorB, Guuao, Iamcuriousblue, Jeff G., JessicaSideways, Kershner, Kootenayvolcano, Lionelt, Mightyfastpig, MishMich, Mynameisnotpj, Natalie Erin, Nfeik, Nietzsche 2, Oldwhore, Peter G Werner, Piechjo, Postcard Cathy, Radagast83, Rakkar, RockfangSemi, Samuel Blanning, SarahEmma, SatyrTN, Scarykitty, Severa, ShelfSkewed, Skoojal, SocratesAD, Themfromspace, Transwarrior, TruthbringerToronto, Tychocat, Waacstats, WikkiBurr, Woohookitty, Xe7al, 22 anonymous edits

Catharine MacKinnon *Source*: http://en.wikipedia.org/w/index.php?oldid=458912234 *Contributors*: 6afraidof7, Adambiswanger1, Ahoerstemeier, Aine63, Alison, Amorrow, Andrewpmk, Andrewsthistle, Andycjp, AnniMars, Antaeus Feldspar, Aphaia, Bluewolverine, Bsktcase, C521, Can't sleep, clown will eat me, Causa sui, Charles Matthews, Chris the speller, Cjs2111, Classicfilms, ConDissenter, Cryptico, Currer1013, CutOffTies, Cybermud, CyntWorkStuff, D6, Dargen, Darklock, Daveman 84, David Gerard, Deepak1621, Dillardjj, DocWatson42, Donfbreed, Dtobias, Eastlaw, El C, Eloquence, Emeraldcityserendipity, Epa101, Epbr123, Epischedda, Esperant, Famspear, Flitzer, FloNight, Fplay, Francium12, GregorB, Grendelkhan, Gurch, Guttlekraw, Heyhey, HighMindOf2, Hmwith, HolidayFever, ISD, Iamcuriousblue, Imeisel, Iridescent, JackofOz, Jdcooper, John Nevard, Johnpacklambert, Jusdafax, K8lj, KGasso, Kablammo, KatharineHepburn, Koavf, Lapaz, Larrybob, LaszloWalrus, Lenticel, Lionelt, Logan, Long lost friend, Mcochs, Metamagician3000, Michael Hardy, Michael L. Kaufman, Mneme33, Nick Levinson, NickBush24, Nicke Lilltroll, Ohnoitsjamie, Owen, Oxo, Paul Barlow, Perardi, Peter G Werner, PinkCake, Pinktulip, Postdlf, Proofchecker1, Pstrandberg, Radgeek, Retodon8, Rich

Image Sources, Licenses and Contributors

Image:Anfem2.svg *Source*: http://en.wikipedia.org/w/index.php?title=File:Anfem2.svg *License*: Public Domain *Contributors*: Liftarn

Image:Anarcha-feminism.svg *Source*: http://en.wikipedia.org/w/index.php?title=File:Anarcha-feminism.svg *License*: Creative Commons Attribution-Sharealike 3.0 *Contributors*: Alexei Yakovlev

File:8La Voz de la Mujer.jpg *Source*: http://en.wikipedia.org/w/index.php?title=File:8La_Voz_de_la_Mujer.jpg *License*: Public Domain *Contributors*: Caetano Bresci, Foroa, Maldonadographics, 2 anonymous edits

Image:Lucifer, The Light-Bearer.jpg *Source*: http://en.wikipedia.org/w/index.php?title=File:Lucifer,_The_Light-Bearer.jpg *License*: Public Domain *Contributors*: Moses Harman, Lillian Harman, Edwin Cox Walker

Image:Mlacerda.png *Source*: http://en.wikipedia.org/w/index.php?title=File:Mlacerda.png *License*: Public Domain *Contributors*: Dodo, Flominator, Koroesu, Mr.Rocks, Mutter Erde, Owen

File:Emma Goldman seated.jpg *Source*: http://en.wikipedia.org/w/index.php?title=File:Emma_Goldman_seated.jpg *License*: Public Domain *Contributors*: T. Kajiwara

Image:EmmaGoldmanQuote2000.JPG *Source*: http://en.wikipedia.org/w/index.php?title=File:EmmaGoldmanQuote2000.JPG *License*: Creative Commons Attribution-Sharealike 3.0 *Contributors*: Carolmooredc

Image:MP 2 tapa grande.gif *Source*: http://en.wikipedia.org/w/index.php?title=File:MP_2_tapa_grande.gif *License*: unknown *Contributors*: N1h11

File:MacKinnon.8May.CambridgeMA.png *Source*: http://en.wikipedia.org/w/index.php?title=File:MacKinnon.8May.CambridgeMA.png *License*: Public Domain *Contributors*: Butko, Crunk, The Honorable, 2 anonymous edits

File:Loudspeaker.svg *Source*: http://en.wikipedia.org/w/index.php?title=File:Loudspeaker.svg *License*: Public Domain *Contributors*: Bayo, Gmaxwell, Husky, Iamunknown, Mirithing, Myself488, Nethac DIU, Omegatron, Rocket000, The Evil IP address, Wouterhagens, 19 anonymous edits

File:Rosetta Reitz.jpg *Source*: http://en.wikipedia.org/w/index.php?title=File:Rosetta_Reitz.jpg *License*: Creative Commons Attribution-Sharealike 3.0 *Contributors*: Rosetta Reitz, Duke University

File:Blues is a woman Reitz.jpg *Source*: http://en.wikipedia.org/w/index.php?title=File:Blues_is_a_woman_Reitz.jpg *License*: Creative Commons Attribution-Sharealike 3.0 *Contributors*: Barbara Weinberg Barefield

File:Rosetta Reitz Closeup.jpg *Source*: http://en.wikipedia.org/w/index.php?title=File:Rosetta_Reitz_Closeup.jpg *License*: Creative Commons Attribution-Sharealike 3.0 *Contributors*: Rosetta Reitz, Duke University

File:Bristol_Hotel_San_Francisco_01.jpg *Source*: http://en.wikipedia.org/w/index.php?title=File:Bristol_Hotel_San_Francisco_01.jpg *License*: Creative Commons Zero *Contributors*: User:Kaldari

File:Gloria Steinem at news conference, Women's Action Alliance, January 12, 1972.jpg *Source*: http://en.wikipedia.org/w/index.php?title=File:Gloria_Steinem_at_news_conference,_Women's_Action_Alliance,_January_12,_1972.jpg *License*: Public Domain *Contributors*: Warren K. Leffler

File:Gloria Steinem 2008 cropped.jpg *Source*: http://en.wikipedia.org/w/index.php?title=File:Gloria_Steinem_2008_cropped.jpg *License*: Creative Commons Attribution 2.0 *Contributors*: Gloria_Steinem_2008.jpg: Mindy Kittay of Boulder, Colorado derivative work: Kaldari (talk)

License

GNU Free Documentation License

A compilation of the Document or its derivatives with other separate and independent documents or works, in or on a volume of a storage or distribution medium, is called an "aggregate" if the copyright resulting from the compilation is not used to limit the legal rights of the compilation's users beyond what the individual works permit. When the Document is included in an aggregate, this License does not apply to the other works in the aggregate which are not themselves derivative works of the Document.

If the Cover Text requirement of section 3 is applicable to these copies of the Document, then if the Document is less than one half of the entire aggregate, the Document's Cover Texts may be placed on covers that bracket the Document within the aggregate, or the electronic equivalent of covers if the Document is in electronic form. Otherwise they must appear on printed covers that bracket the whole aggregate.

8. TRANSLATION

Translation is considered a kind of modification, so you may distribute translations of the Document under the terms of section 4. Replacing Invariant Sections with translations requires special permission from their copyright holders, but you may include translations of some or all Invariant Sections in addition to the original versions of these Invariant Sections. You may include a translation of this License, and all the license notices in the Document, and any Warranty Disclaimers, provided that you also include the original English version of this License and the original versions of those notices and disclaimers. In case of a disagreement between the translation and the original version of this License or a notice or disclaimer, the original version will prevail.

If a section in the Document is Entitled "Acknowledgements", "Dedications", or "History", the requirement (section 4) to Preserve its Title (section 1) will typically require changing the actual title.

9. TERMINATION

You may not copy, modify, sublicense, or distribute the Document except as expressly provided under this License. Any attempt otherwise to copy, modify, sublicense, or distribute it is void, and will automatically terminate your rights under this License.

However, if you cease all violation of this License, then your license from a particular copyright holder is reinstated (a) provisionally, unless and until the copyright holder explicitly and finally terminates your license, and (b) permanently, if the copyright holder fails to notify you of the violation by some reasonable means prior to 60 days after the cessation.

Moreover, your license from a particular copyright holder is reinstated permanently if the copyright holder notifies you of the violation by some reasonable means, this is the first time you have received notice of violation of this License (for any work) from that copyright holder, and you cure the violation prior to 30 days after your receipt of the notice.

Termination of your rights under this section does not terminate the licenses of parties who have received copies or rights from you under this License. If your rights have been terminated and not permanently reinstated, receipt of a copy of some or all of the same material does not give you any rights to use it.

10. FUTURE REVISIONS OF THIS LICENSE

The Free Software Foundation may publish new, revised versions of the GNU Free Documentation License from time to time. Such new versions will be similar in spirit to the present version, but may differ in detail to address new problems or concerns. See http://www.gnu.org/copyleft/.

Each version of the License is given a distinguishing version number. If the Document specifies that a particular numbered version of this License "or any later version" applies to it, you have the option of following the terms and conditions either of that specified version or of any later version that has been published (not as a draft) by the Free Software Foundation. If the Document does not specify a version number of this License, you may choose any version ever published (not as a draft) by the Free Software Foundation. If the Document specifies that a proxy can decide which future versions of this License can be used, that proxy's public statement of acceptance of a version permanently authorizes you to choose that version for the Document.

11. RELICENSING

"Massive Multiauthor Collaboration Site" (or "MMC Site") means any World Wide Web server that publishes copyrightable works and also provides prominent facilities for anybody to edit those works. A public wiki that anybody can edit is an example of such a server. A "Massive Multiauthor Collaboration" (or "MMC") contained in the site means any set of copyrightable works thus published on the MMC site.

"CC-BY-SA" means the Creative Commons Attribution-Share Alike 3.0 license published by Creative Commons Corporation, a not-for-profit corporation with a principal place of business in San Francisco, California, as well as future copyleft versions of that license published by that same organization.

"Incorporate" means to publish or republish a Document, in whole or in part, as part of another Document.

An MMC is "eligible for relicensing" if it is licensed under this License, and if all works that were first published under this License somewhere other than this MMC, and subsequently incorporated in whole or in part into the MMC, (1) had no cover texts or invariant sections, and (2) were thus incorporated prior to November 1, 2008.

The operator of an MMC Site may republish an MMC contained in the site under CC-BY-SA on the same site at any time before August 1, 2009, provided the MMC is eligible for relicensing.

How to use this License for your documents

To use this License in a document you have written, include a copy of the License in the document and put the following copyright and license notices just after the title page:

Copyright (c) YEAR YOUR NAME.

Permission is granted to copy, distribute and/or modify this document

under the terms of the GNU Free Documentation License, Version 1.3

or any later version published by the Free Software Foundation;

with no Invariant Sections, no Front-Cover Texts, and no Back-Cover Texts.

A copy of the license is included in the section entitled "GNU

Free Documentation License".

If you have Invariant Sections, Front-Cover Texts and Back-Cover Texts, replace the "with...Texts." line with this:

with the Invariant Sections being LIST THEIR TITLES, with the

Front-Cover Texts being LIST, and with the Back-Cover Texts being LIST.

If you have Invariant Sections without Cover Texts, or some other combination of the three, merge those two alternatives to suit the situation.

If your document contains nontrivial examples of program code, we recommend releasing these examples in parallel under your choice of free software license, such as the GNU General Public License, to permit their use in free software.

Creative Commons Attribution-ShareAlike 3.0 Unported License

CREATIVE COMMONS CORPORATION IS NOT A LAW FIRM AND DOES NOT PROVIDE LEGAL SERVICES. DISTRIBUTION OF THIS LICENSE DOES NOT CREATE AN ATTORNEY-CLIENT RELATIONSHIP. CREATIVE COMMONS PROVIDES THIS INFORMATION ON AN «AS-IS» BASIS. CREATIVE COMMONS MAKES NO WARRANTIES REGARDING THE INFORMATION PROVIDED, AND DISCLAIMS LIABILITY FOR DAMAGES RESULTING FROM ITS USE.

License

THE WORK (AS DEFINED BELOW) IS PROVIDED UNDER THE TERMS OF THIS CREATIVE COMMONS PUBLIC LICENSE («CCPL» OR «LICENSE»). THE WORK IS PROTECTED BY COPYRIGHT AND/OR OTHER APPLICABLE LAW. ANY USE OF THE WORK OTHER THAN AS AUTHORIZED UNDER THIS LICENSE OR COPYRIGHT LAW IS PROHIBITED.

BY EXERCISING ANY RIGHTS TO THE WORK PROVIDED HERE, YOU ACCEPT AND AGREE TO BE BOUND BY THE TERMS OF THIS LICENSE. TO THE EXTENT THIS LICENSE MAY BE CONSIDERED TO BE A CONTRACT, THE LICENSOR GRANTS YOU THE RIGHTS CONTAINED HERE IN CONSIDERATION OF YOUR ACCEPTANCE OF SUCH TERMS AND CONDITIONS.

1. Definitions

"Adaptation" means a work based upon the Work, or upon the Work and other pre-existing works, such as a translation, adaptation, derivative work, arrangement of music or other alterations of a literary or artistic work, or phonogram or performance and includes cinematographic adaptations or any other form in which the Work may be recast, transformed, or adapted including in any form recognizably derived from the original, except that a work that constitutes a Collection will not be considered an Adaptation for the purpose of this License. For the avoidance of doubt, where the Work is a musical work, performance or phonogram, the synchronization of the Work in timed-relation with a moving image ("synching") will be considered an Adaptation for the purpose of this License.

"Collection" means a collection of literary or artistic works, such as encyclopedias and anthologies, or performances, phonograms or broadcasts, or other works or subject matter other than works listed in Section 1(f) below, which, by reason of the selection and arrangement of their contents, constitute intellectual creations, in which the Work is included in its entirety in unmodified form along with one or more other contributions, each constituting separate and independent works in themselves, which together are assembled into a collective whole. A work that constitutes a Collection will not be considered an Adaptation (as defined below) for the purposes of this License.

"Creative Commons Compatible License" means a license that is listed at http://creativecommons.org/compatiblelicenses that has been approved by Creative Commons as being essentially equivalent to this License, including, at a minimum, because that license: (i) contains terms that have the same purpose, meaning and effect as the License Elements of this License; and, (ii) explicitly permits the relicensing of adaptations of works made available under that license under this License or a Creative Commons jurisdiction license with the same License Elements as this License.

"Distribute" means to make available to the public the original and copies of the Work or Adaptation, as appropriate, through sale or other transfer of ownership.

"License Elements" means the following high-level license attributes as selected by Licensor and indicated in the title of this License: Attribution, ShareAlike.

"Licensor" means the individual, individuals, entity or entities that offer(s) the Work under the terms of this License.

"Original Author" means, in the case of a literary or artistic work, the individual, individuals, entity or entities who created the Work or if no individual or entity can be identified, the publisher; and in addition (i) in the case of a performance the actors, singers, musicians, dancers, and other persons who act, sing, deliver, declaim, play in, interpret or otherwise perform literary or artistic works or expressions of folklore; (ii) in the case of a phonogram the producer being the person or legal entity who first fixes the sounds of a performance or other sounds; and, (iii) in the case of broadcasts, the organization that transmits the broadcast.

"Work" means the literary and/or artistic work offered under the terms of this License including without limitation any production in the literary, scientific and artistic domain, whatever may be the mode or form of its expression including digital form, such as a book, pamphlet and other writing; a lecture, address, sermon or other work of the same nature; a dramatic or dramatico-musical work; a choreographic work or entertainment in dumb show; a musical composition with or without words; a cinematographic work to which are assimilated works expressed by a process analogous to cinematography; a work of drawing, painting, architecture, sculpture, engraving or lithography; a photographic work to which are assimilated works expressed by a process analogous to photography; a work of applied art; an illustration, map, plan, sketch or three-dimensional work relative to geography, topography, architecture or science; a performance; a broadcast; a phonogram; a compilation of data to the extent it is protected as a copyrightable work; or a work performed by a variety or circus performer to the extent it is not otherwise considered a literary or artistic work.

"You" means an individual or entity exercising rights under this License who has not previously violated the terms of this License with respect to the Work, or who has received express permission from the Licensor to exercise rights under this License despite a previous violation.

"Publicly Perform" means to perform public recitations of the Work and to communicate to the public those public recitations, by any means or process, including by wire or wireless means or public digital performances; to make available to the public Works in such a way that members of the public may access these Works from a place and at a place individually chosen by them; to perform the Work to the public by any means or process and the communication to the public of the performances of the Work, including by public digital performance; to broadcast and rebroadcast the Work by any means including signs, sounds or images.

"Reproduce" means to make copies of the Work by any means including without limitation by sound or visual recordings and the right of fixation and reproducing fixations of the Work, including storage of a protected performance or phonogram in digital form or other electronic medium.

2. Fair Dealing Rights

Nothing in this License is intended to reduce, limit, or restrict any uses free from copyright or rights arising from limitations or exceptions that are provided for in connection with the copyright protection under copyright law or other applicable laws.

3. License Grant

Subject to the terms and conditions of this License, Licensor hereby grants You a worldwide, royalty-free, non-exclusive, perpetual (for the duration of the applicable copyright) license to exercise the rights in the Work as stated below:

a. to Reproduce the Work, to incorporate the Work into one or more Collections, and to Reproduce the Work as incorporated in the Collections;

b. to create and Reproduce Adaptations provided that any such Adaptation, including any translation in any medium, takes reasonable steps to clearly label, demarcate or otherwise identify that changes were made to the original Work. For example, a translation could be marked "The original work was translated from English to Spanish," or a modification could indicate "The original work has been modified.";

c. to Distribute and Publicly Perform the Work including as incorporated in Collections; and,

d. to Distribute and Publicly Perform Adaptations.

e. For the avoidance of doubt:

    vi. **Non-waivable Compulsory License Schemes.** In those jurisdictions in which the right to collect royalties through any statutory or compulsory licensing scheme cannot be waived, the Licensor reserves the exclusive right to collect such royalties for any exercise by You of the rights granted under this License;

    vii. **Waivable Compulsory License Schemes.** In those jurisdictions in which the right to collect royalties through any statutory or compulsory licensing scheme can be waived, the Licensor waives the exclusive right to collect such royalties for any exercise by You of the rights granted under this License; and,

    viii. **Voluntary License Schemes.** The Licensor waives the right to collect royalties, whether individually or, in the event that the Licensor is a member of a collecting society that administers voluntary licensing schemes, via that society, from any exercise by You of the rights granted under this License.

The above rights may be exercised in all media and formats whether now known or hereafter devised. The above rights include the right to make such modifications as are technically necessary to exercise the rights in other media and formats. Subject to Section 8(f), all rights not expressly granted by Licensor are hereby reserved.

4. Restrictions

The license granted in Section 3 above is expressly made subject to and limited by the following restrictions:

a.   You may Distribute or Publicly Perform the Work only under the terms of this License. You must include a copy of, or the Uniform Resource Identifier (URI) for, this License with every copy of the Work You Distribute or Publicly Perform. You may not offer or impose any terms on the Work that restrict the terms of this License or the ability of the recipient of the Work to exercise the rights granted to that recipient under the terms of the License. You may not sublicense the Work. You must keep intact all notices that refer to this License and to the disclaimer of warranties with every copy of the Work You Distribute or Publicly Perform. When You Distribute or Publicly Perform the Work, You may not impose any effective technological measures on the Work that restrict the ability of a recipient of the Work from You to exercise the rights granted to that recipient under the terms of the License. This Section 4(a) applies to the Work as incorporated in a Collection, but this does not require the Collection apart from the Work itself to be made subject to the terms of this License. If You create a Collection, upon notice from any Licensor You must, to the extent practicable, remove from the Collection any credit as required by Section 4(c), as requested. If You create an Adaptation, upon notice from any Licensor You must, to the extent practicable, remove from the Adaptation any credit as required by Section 4(c), as requested.

b.   You may Distribute or Publicly Perform an Adaptation only under the terms of: (i) this License; (ii) a later version of this License with the same License Elements as this License; (iii) a Creative Commons jurisdiction license (either this or a later license version) that contains the same License Elements as this License (e.g., Attribution-ShareAlike 3.0 US)); (iv) a Creative Commons Compatible License. If you license the Adaptation under one of the licenses mentioned in (iv), you must comply with the terms of that license. If you license the Adaptation under the terms of any of the licenses mentioned in (i), (ii) or (iii) (the "Applicable License"), you must comply with the terms of the Applicable License generally and the following provisions: (I) You must include a copy of, or the URI for, the Applicable License with every copy of each Adaptation You Distribute or Publicly Perform; (II) You may not offer or impose any terms on the Adaptation that restrict the terms of the Applicable License or the ability of the recipient of the Adaptation to exercise the rights granted to that recipient under the terms of the Applicable License; (III) You must keep intact all notices that refer to the Applicable License and to the disclaimer of warranties with every copy of the Work as included in the Adaptation You Distribute or Publicly Perform; (IV) when You Distribute or Publicly Perform the Adaptation, You may not impose any effective technological measures on the Adaptation that restrict the ability of a recipient of the Adaptation from You to exercise the rights granted to that recipient under the terms of the Applicable License. This Section 4(b) applies to the Adaptation as incorporated in a Collection, but this does not require the Collection apart from the Adaptation itself to be made subject to the terms of the Applicable License.

c.   If You Distribute, or Publicly Perform the Work or any Adaptations or Collections, You must, unless a request has been made pursuant to Section 4(a), keep intact all copyright notices for the Work and provide, reasonable to the medium or means You are utilizing: (i) the name of the Original Author (or pseudonym, if applicable) if supplied, and/or if the Original Author and/or Licensor designate another party or parties (e.g., a sponsor institute, publishing entity, journal) for attribution ("Attribution Parties") in Licensor's copyright notice, terms of service or by other reasonable means, the name of such party or parties; (ii) the title of the Work if supplied; (iii) to the extent reasonably practicable, the URI, if any, that Licensor specifies to be associated with the Work, unless such URI does not refer to the copyright notice or licensing information for the Work; and (iv) , consistent with Section 3(b), in the case of an Adaptation, a credit identifying the use of the Work in the Adaptation (e.g., "French translation of the Work by Original Author," or "Screenplay based on original Work by Original Author"). The credit required by this Section 4(c) may be implemented in any reasonable manner; provided, however, that in the case of a Adaptation or Collection, at a minimum such credit will appear, if a credit for all contributing authors of the Adaptation or Collection appears, then as part of these credits and in a manner at least as prominent as the credits for the other contributing authors. For the avoidance of doubt, You may only use the credit required by this Section for the purpose of attribution in the manner set out above and, by exercising Your rights under this License, You may not implicitly or explicitly assert or imply any connection with, sponsorship or endorsement by the Original Author, Licensor and/or Attribution Parties, as appropriate, of You or Your use of the Work, without the separate, express prior written permission of the Original Author, Licensor and/or Attribution Parties.

d.   Except as otherwise agreed in writing by the Licensor or as may be otherwise permitted by applicable law, if You Reproduce, Distribute or Publicly Perform the Work either by itself or as part of any Adaptations

or Collections, You must not distort, mutilate, modify or take other derogatory action in relation to the Work which would be prejudicial to the Original Author's honor or reputation. Licensor agrees that in those jurisdictions (e.g. Japan), in which any exercise of the right granted in Section 3(b) of this License (the right to make Adaptations) would be deemed to be a distortion, mutilation, modification or other derogatory action prejudicial to the Original Author's honor and reputation, the Licensor will waive or not assert, as appropriate, this Section, to the fullest extent permitted by the applicable national law, to enable You to reasonably exercise Your right under Section 3(b) of this License (right to make Adaptations) but not otherwise.

5. Representations, Warranties and Disclaimer

UNLESS OTHERWISE MUTUALLY AGREED TO BY THE PARTIES IN WRITING, LICENSOR OFFERS THE WORK AS-IS AND MAKES NO REPRESENTATIONS OR WARRANTIES OF ANY KIND CONCERNING THE WORK, EXPRESS, IMPLIED, STATUTORY OR OTHERWISE, INCLUDING, WITHOUT LIMITATION, WARRANTIES OF TITLE, MERCHANTIBILITY, FITNESS FOR A PARTICULAR PURPOSE, NONINFRINGEMENT, OR THE ABSENCE OF LATENT OR OTHER DEFECTS, ACCURACY, OR THE PRESENCE OF ABSENCE OF ERRORS, WHETHER OR NOT DISCOVERABLE. SOME JURISDICTIONS DO NOT ALLOW THE EXCLUSION OF IMPLIED WARRANTIES, SO SUCH EXCLUSION MAY NOT APPLY TO YOU.

6. Limitation on Liability

EXCEPT TO THE EXTENT REQUIRED BY APPLICABLE LAW, IN NO EVENT WILL LICENSOR BE LIABLE TO YOU ON ANY LEGAL THEORY FOR ANY SPECIAL, INCIDENTAL, CONSEQUENTIAL, PUNITIVE OR EXEMPLARY DAMAGES ARISING OUT OF THIS LICENSE OR THE USE OF THE WORK, EVEN IF LICENSOR HAS BEEN ADVISED OF THE POSSIBILITY OF SUCH DAMAGES.

7. Termination

a.   This License and the rights granted hereunder will terminate automatically upon any breach by You of the terms of this License. Individuals or entities who have received Adaptations or Collections from You under this License, however, will not have their licenses terminated provided such individuals or entities remain in full compliance with those licenses. Sections 1, 2, 5, 6, 7, and 8 will survive any termination of this License.

b.   Subject to the above terms and conditions, the license granted here is perpetual (for the duration of the applicable copyright in the Work). Notwithstanding the above, Licensor reserves the right to release the Work under different license terms or to stop distributing the Work at any time; provided, however that any such election will not serve to withdraw this License (or any other license that has been, or is required to be, granted under the terms of this License), and this License will continue in full force and effect unless terminated as stated above.

8. Miscellaneous

a.   Each time You Distribute or Publicly Perform the Work or a Collection, the Licensor offers to the recipient a license to the Work on the same terms and conditions as the license granted to You under this License.

b.   Each time You Distribute or Publicly Perform an Adaptation, Licensor offers to the recipient a license to the original Work on the same terms and conditions as the license granted to You under this License.

c.   If any provision of this License is invalid or unenforceable under applicable law, it shall not affect the validity or enforceability of the remainder of the terms of this License, and without further action by the parties to this agreement, such provision shall be reformed to the minimum extent necessary to make such provision valid and enforceable.

d.   No term or provision of this License shall be deemed waived and no breach consented to unless such waiver or consent shall be in writing and signed by the party to be charged with such waiver or consent.

e.   This License constitutes the entire agreement between the parties with respect to the Work licensed here. There are no understandings, agreements or representations with respect to the Work not specified here. Licensor shall not be bound by any additional provisions that may appear in any communication from You. This License may not be modified without the mutual written agreement of the Licensor and You.

f.   The rights granted under, and the subject matter referenced, in this License were drafted utilizing the terminology of the Berne Convention for the Protection of Literary and Artistic Works (as amended on September 28, 1979), the Rome Convention of 1961, the WIPO Copyright Treaty of 1996, the WIPO Performances and Phonograms Treaty of 1996 and the Universal Copyright Convention (as revised on July 24, 1971). These rights and subject matter take effect in the relevant jurisdiction in which the License terms are sought to be enforced according to the corresponding provisions of the implementation of those treaty provisions in the applicable national law. If the standard suite of rights granted under applicable copyright law includes additional rights not granted under this License, such additional rights are deemed to be included in the License; this License is not intended to restrict the license of any rights under applicable law.

Lightning Source UK Ltd.
Milton Keynes UK
UKOW04f2159190916

283362UK00007B/191/P